Creating Change for Vulnerable Teens

Creating Change for Vulnerable Teens

*Lessons from a Therapeutic
Farm Making a Difference to
the Lives of Young People*

TISH FEILDEN

Foreword by Jonathan Dimbleby

Jessica Kingsley Publishers
London and Philadelphia

First published in Great Britain in 2021 by Jessica Kingsley Publishers
An Hachette Company

1

Copyright © Tish Feilden 2021
Foreword copyright © Jonathan Dimbleby 2021

Front cover image source: Jamie's Farm.

A CIP catalogue record for this title is available from the
British Library and the Library of Congress

ISBN 978 1 78775 536 9
eISBN 978 1 78775 537 6

Printed and bound in Great Britain by Clays Ltd

Jessica Kingsley Publishers' policy is to use papers that are natural,
renewable and recyclable products and made from wood grown in
sustainable forests. The logging and manufacturing processes are expected
to conform to the environmental regulations of the country of origin.

Jessica Kingsley Publishers
73 Collier Street
London N1 9BE, UK

www.jkp.com

Contents

Foreword

Tish Feilden has written an inspirational book. Understanding, compassion and wisdom illuminate every paragraph in this account of her role as 'Therapeutic Lead' at a charity which provides a unique rural environment in which to support troubled teenagers in need of love, support and professional understanding. Feilden is a renowned psychotherapist who wears her knowledge and expertise lightly. Hers is not a 'teach yourself' book and it is mercifully free of 'psycho-babble'. It is impossible to turn its pages without learning huge amounts about young people and about ourselves.

I had the privilege of playing a small part at the birth of Jamie's Farm, which was founded in 2006 by Tish and her son, Jamie, to realize their shared passion to make a difference to the lives of inner-city teenagers whose futures are blighted by violence, crime and fear. I have seen their vision develop from small beginnings to the point where, demand from secondary schools is now so great, the charity has expanded to five farms (one of which is in the heart of London). It is an astonishing achievement and of immense social value. In these pages we learn about how this has been achieved and why it works.

One of the delights is to 'meet' in these pages many of those young people who have 'found themselves' at Jamie's Farm and to hear, through their voices, why it has been such a life-changing experience. By learning to care for farm animals and sharing their lives with one another in a unique family atmosphere, we discover how their self-awareness and self-esteem blossom. As Feilden writes, young people 'have a yearning to be understood, the desire to be loving and loveable, and most of all to be different, a "better", happier version of themselves'.

The book ranges widely to explore – in language that is vivid, clear and free of jargon – the unique set of pressures that teenagers face in the 21st century. We learn about the confusion and anxiety these pressures can cause and how they may trigger antisocial defence mechanisms that – if adults respond with greater understanding and empathy – can be gently overcome to be replaced by the positive and enjoyable relationships that most of us crave.

There is no sentimentality in these pages. The Feildens, supported by trained colleagues, have established protocols under which everyone is treated as an individual but has to behave responsibly as a member of the group. There are rows and conflicts, shouting and tears – emotional outbursts which have to be mediated calmly but firmly. There are clear rules (for example, no phones, no sweets and no smoking) that establish protective boundaries which provide the security that vulnerable young people crave.

The scholarship which underpins this approach is impressive, but the success of Jamie's Farm springs from the fact that the team really cares about the troubled young lives that are entrusted to them. The atmosphere that this generates exudes a very special kind of generosity, happiness and love.

The proof of the Jamie's Farm pudding is in its results: huge reductions in school exclusions, a sharp drop in gang membership, far less truancy and much greater 'positivity' – one of Feilden's lodestar terms.

I found *Creating Change for Vulnerable Teens* as illuminating as it was gripping. If you are a parent, a carer or a teacher, I am sure that you will have a similar response. But you don't need to be in any of those roles to be stimulated, entertained, touched and influenced by the wisdom that shines from every page. Enjoy!

Jonathan Dimbleby
Broadcaster and author

Introduction

In at the deep end

A fraught night with arguing, shouting, claims of injustice and counter recrimination between the members of the group. It is, thankfully, sunny, which helps the spirits, but I have not slept. A group has come to stay on our small family farm, hoping it will give them a break from their disruptive patterns at school and the stresses of family and cultural life. They are mostly Year 9 and 10, some have 'hard' exteriors, some are more obviously vulnerable, but in this unfamiliar place they look to each other for support or diversion. Arguments last night led to someone throwing an MP3 player into the nettles; it was never found, tempers flared, language was florid, and generally this morning they are grumpy and resentful, tired and fed up. Their verdict is they hated camping in the field and want to go home.

I have been racking my brains all night about how best to deal with this. I am a great believer that 'threats can become opportunities' or grist for the mill. It was never going to be a smooth ride, but the reactions of the young people last night are telling me something. I just need to try and understand. I am regretting we assumed they would enjoy camping, and wishing we had had a level playing field, either us all in tents, or all in the house. Too late, I recognize that the young teaching assistant who accompanied them is ambivalent herself about being in the farm. She was keen to camp and supervise the girls, but understandably upset when things got out of hand. Her distress fed the young people's. This whole experience of coming to a farm in Wiltshire is way outside their comfort zones in its unfamiliarity. Possibly it is even scary! These young people live in a troubled neighbourhood in Hackney where there are lots of gangs and street violence. Camping in the dark, with physical discomfort – maybe that was too much. It did not signal safety, or nurture, or care. Yet, the stretch, being in the unknown, the risk of leaving familiarity, is that always a bad thing? This morning is critical. We need to talk, but most of all we need to listen and we want them to want to stay.

First things first, we cook a big breakfast together, some of the group feed the animals, and we sit down as a 'family', and try to recalibrate. They are well fed, seated around the table, some slouching, some facing away, one knuckle-gnawing, another hiding behind a curtain of hair, and I am thinking they are expecting a lecture on their misdemeanours. 'OK,' I say. 'We want this to be a good experience for you and we have got off to a bad start. Firstly, we need to apologize. We got it wrong. We assumed you would like camping. I am sorry. That was an error, a misjudgement, and this we can change. Everyone who wants to can sleep in the house. Arguing into the night, however, that is horrible for you, and for us, and that is not acceptable.

Precious things, such as phones, are likely to cause problems and that is why these need to be handed in for safekeeping. But enough from me, let us start again, draw a line in the sand and be on the same side. I would like to hear from you. Let's go around the table, adults included, and say something we could have done differently last night.'

To my relief each and every person spoke about their regrets and acknowledged what they could have done to make for a better experience. It did not become a tit-for-tat conversation; they did their apologizing, to each other, and to us, knowing that there was then a definite full stop. By a hair's breadth there was a big enough part of each individual that wanted this to work and was willing to give it a go. We needed to get on with it, get outside, to 'get stuck in' (to use their words), not linger in the conflict. It would not be plain sailing, and if they were really going to let us know them, that would include them testing us out. As adults, a team, a 'family', we needed to believe in them, stay positive and be consistent and clear.

I recognized that by getting on that bus to leave Hackney yesterday, these young people had shown that there was a greater part of themselves that wanted change and that they were willing to risk the unknown. By Friday we had survived, had fun, been moved and frustrated, challenged and delighted, but the question remained: what then? During the visit, a short film had been made for us all to preserve our memories of the visit. Unbeknown to us, the young people had had open and reflective conversation with the cameraman. We were amazed and surprised. They spoke with such feeling and taught us that the week had really impacted on them, that they felt it was important, and that it would in their words lead to them changing their attitudes and behaviours, back at school and in their families. We had jumped in at the deep end but, thankfully, had survived.

The following are quotes from this film, *Life Outside Hackney*:[1]

- 'They treat you like family and put the parts of you together.'

- 'I realize I was a teacher's worst nightmare.'

- 'Now, I am going to stop and think.'

- 'You can trust them.'

It is now ten years on, and we have formed a charity, Jamie's Farm, and worked with 7000 children in over 650 residential visits across our four residential farms in Bath, Monmouth, Hereford and Lewes, and non-residential farm in Waterloo, London. Our intention has been to intervene preventatively in young lives where the signals have been that these children might otherwise fail to thrive. In our work we hear more frequently from teachers who are worried their pupils are increasingly suffering from mental health problems like self-harming, eating disorders and depression. We are hearing from teachers, parents and practitioners that CAMHS waiting lists are getting longer. Many of these children have previously been flagged up by their schools as vulnerable, but the schools are not resourced to meet the children's needs.

....

1   W. James (producer) (2008) 'Life Outside Hackney' (video of the first visit to Jamie's Farm). Available at www.youtube.com/watch?v=iTyXXovYd00 (accessed 31/ 0 1/2020).

Another group of children who are particularly vulnerable are those who escalate their behaviour as a cry for help; tragically too many end up excluded as the schools cannot cope with their impact on the learning of others. As a society, we need to help, and Jamie's Farm has shown that intensive intervention can reroute these children and redirect them back to their potential. There is a lot to share, from our experiences, from the young people speaking for themselves, and also from relating this to the great body of knowledge that is growing daily about the stage of adolescence: about how adolescents' brains are changing, how today's culture is affecting them, and how their behaviour is in itself a communication and is driven by their defences.

Overall it is a good news story. I hope if you read this book you will feel immersed and absorbed by the narratives, but also come away at the end feeling you have the tools and understanding to enjoy living or working with your teenagers better.

Behind every book and its author there is a story and a motivation to write. My earlier life had felt unremarkable in its absence of drama or huge difficulties. I grew up in Africa and as an adult wanted to work with children who were struggling. As a 'rescuer' at this stage, I did not recognize that my own motivation came from the script set in motion early in my life of feeling I had to be the family member who soothed troubled waters. At first I worked as a teacher, and in particular I was drawn to special education with boys who back then in the 1970s were labelled 'maladjusted'; bright but disturbed children who had bundles of problems, and could not manage or be managed in mainstream schools. I loved working with them, but while I concurrently was studying for a PhD, I realized I needed to understand more. I went on to become a psychotherapist and, 25 years later, when I was often supporting schools and teachers, supervising school counsellors, and was a mother of three children and foster mother to one, suddenly my life changed.

The second chapter of my life and the real inspiration for this book came unexpectedly. In 2005 I found my husband, my lifelong friend and partner in life, dead under a tree he had cut down. Richard, having fulfilled his dream of owning some woodland, was clearing a glade when he cut a large ash tree that sprang back, fell, and took the life from him. For the next few days I was in shock. I am grateful for the way the body and mind have the ability to numb and dumb themselves as a way to cope with intolerable pain. I was also grateful for being a psychotherapist, as I could almost watch, from a bird's eye place in my head, my own process of grieving. I could carry on as if life was normal and then break down at the supermarket counter; I could hear a piece of music and want to wail; my rage could burst the dam with unexpected triggers; or I could carry on working, living a bit like a zombie, just to keep things on an even keel. Understanding myself a bit, and the wonderful love of friends, the bond with my children and our shared lives, made the days pass without being engulfed and swept away in despair.

When there is a crater in your life there is an instinct to fill it. Tragedy can become opportunity and I, like many grieving people, jumped into the space. Together with my son Jamie, with a synergy of need, interest and enthusiasm, I started inviting groups, like the one described above, to stay on our small farm.

Jamie had his own story that played a strong motivating part in his creation of the charity. He had grown up with a passion for farming. By the age of 14 he had 60 animals all under his sole care. He borrowed land, bought and sold, bred and bartered, and worked tirelessly with sheep, pigs and cattle. In every spare moment, he helped a neighbouring farmer, who along with *Farmers Weekly* – all he ever read – taught him everything he knew. His father was rather dismayed. He was an architect, with no interest in farming, and wished that Jamie, a bright boy, but one who hated school, would turn his head to medicine, or at the very least veterinary medicine. In today's terms, Jamie's behaviour reminds me of children who are currently diagnosed with attention deficit hyperactivity disorder (ADHD). Sitting at a desk all day simply did not, and does not, work for him. Farming, chopping logs, going on long hikes, relating to people and knowing how to have fun with children, all made him happy. In retrospect, I am thankful that he did not get the grades needed for medicine but on graduation with a degree in History he became one of the first cohort selected to do Teach First[2] in 2003. Thrown in at the deep end of teaching, facing groups of angry, frustrated pupils, disengaged from formal learning, who were facing a downward spiral, he recognized that many young people were like he had been, but less lucky, struggling with school and home life, failing to find meaning or recognition. Might they flourish and thrive in different settings? He had produced a plan for a mini MBA with Teach First which involved bringing city children into farming, and so we took the plunge and invited a group to come and live and work with us at our small farm for a week. The effects on the children, and the

....

2   Teach First is a social enterprise aiming to address educational disadvantage in England and Wales with its selection of good-quality graduates to do an employment-based teacher training.

way they described the changes they felt happening to them, amazed us, and their teachers.

With enthusiasm, and maybe some necessary naivety, we invited 35 groups of around ten children for a week at a time, with their teachers, living in our home. We worked, cooked, gardened, farmed, played and did a lot of reflection and talking along the way. It quickly became evident that the blend of family life, a therapeutic programme and practical farming allowed children to gradually leave behind their defensive attitudes and emerge into hardworking, caring and intelligent people. We lived and worked all week with a group, but it was the shared passion, positivity and joy that made it all possible. Two remarkable young women from Teach First, Ruth Carney and Jane Brinson, worked alongside us and helped us establish as a charity. We struggled to find a name, so stuck with what the children called it, 'Jamie's Farm'. As a team, we covered different bases but, as friends and colleagues, we shared a lot of fun, positivity and collaboration, alongside the hard work. The change in the children was the reward in itself. They seemed to relax and change shape in the climate of trust and positivity, which took away the stresses of their homes, school life and wider environments.

As former teachers, we were familiar with many of the pressures of school and wanted to form a bridge between their worlds, involving their teachers to help build sustaining relationships that could transfer between the farm and life back at home and school. The teachers who came with the children shared, and were part of, the adventure, the life of the group, the positive change, and their involvement was an essential part of the indelible memories created by the young people. Feeling trustworthy and having developed more trust in others changed what I like to think of as the shape of the children. They felt liked and likeable. They would no longer fit into the jigsaw of previous negative patterns that had sculpted them. As they changed shape, so systemically the relationships with their school would have to shift to accommodate this change. Whereas some of them might have regarded their teachers as hostile, or unapproachable, now the young people had a chance to see them as potentially helpful, on their side, and avail themselves of some of the support that was available that they had previously mistrusted. On return to school the teachers could act as ambassadors for the individuals who they had lived and worked with, carrying the narrative, the abilities and qualities that the young people had, but above all conveying to the other staff a new faith and belief in their potential, helping them see that the train tracks had indeed changed and new, better horizons could be in sight.

Ten years on, there are five farms taking weekly groups of children from various schools, and we have worked with thousands of children. Aside from the four residential farms in Hereford, Monmouth, Lewes and Bath, there is another residential non-residential farm in Waterloo, London. The need is immense: schools are telling us they are struggling with huge numbers of disaffected children, poor attendance, poor relationships with teachers and too high exclusion rates. We are only touching the tip of the iceberg; but the transformation in the teenagers who came to the first Jamie's Farm has led to the development of four more farms. We share the methodology with others, try to enrich the teachers in terms of their own professional development, attend to the culture of the charity as an organization and hope that, with funding and support, more provision can be made The children referred are mostly 11–16, and from all kinds of backgrounds and localities. All of them share a lack of confidence and are failing to thrive. Building trust in their relationships can be the way forward, and they flourish in smaller groups with the chance to be better known as individuals. The teenagers themselves have proven that it is possible to change the script if the right opportunities come along. Advances in neuroscience confirm that the brain at this age is growing and changing at a phenomenal rate.[3] Although our work takes place on farms, the qualities of building potential and positive relationships can happen anywhere: at home, in the classroom or in the social sphere. It is helpful if, as adults, we are familiar with how their defence mechanisms get activated and recognize that 'bad' behaviour is often a symptom, not a cause. They learn through role modelling. If we are helping children to manage their lives better and build self-esteem, I think we need to include their peers and give them a sense of community. Adults need to be inspirational, nurturing but challenging, as children grow through seeing examples of what they might aspire to.

Jamie's Farm: building confidence, self-awareness and resilience

Who comes, what we do and the methodology in a nutshell

Listening to teachers, we hear how they are doing their level best to help vulnerable pupils, but they feel under pressure to

----

3   Newport Academy (2018) 'The facts about teen brain development.' Available at www.newportacademy.com/resources/mental-health/teen-brain-development (accessed 07/04/2020).

fulfil academic attainment targets set by Ofsted and they speak about the struggle to meet the social and psychological needs of struggling pupils alongside their cognitive development. Many schools formerly had school counsellors and this seems to be a diminishing resource, while waiting lists for help for children through CAMHS are growing. Sometimes their structures and staffing levels just cannot meet the diverse needs of their children. Sometimes the children need an intensive experience away from their usual pressures to remodel themselves and make a fresh start.

Children who are failing to thrive in school are referred for a five-day residential experience at Jamie's Farm. Some who have mental health issues are fragile and in need of interventions, but the schools themselves and the mental health service are over-stretched and unable to meet their needs. Young Minds looked at data from HJS (Health Service Journal)[4] which shows that hundreds of children are waiting more than a year for CAMHS treatment, and our visiting teachers are often anxious that their pupils who are struggling with mental health cannot get the support they need. Some lack engagement, and some present with learning difficulties and are now better described as being neurodivergent.[5] The majority of these children have ADHD or autism spectrum disorder (ASD), which make thriving in

....

4   Young Minds (2018a) 'New Figures on CAMHS Waiting Times.' Available at https:// youngminds.org.uk/blog/new-figures-on-camhs-waiting-times (accessed 17/06/2020).

5   Previously, children were diagnosed as having ADHD, autism, oppositional defiant disorder (ODD), or many other ways in which they have special educational needs, but now the term 'neurodivergent' has come into use as a more positive way of looking at different ways in which the brain can be wired and lead to divergent ways of thinking.

mainstream school challenging. Some are in care with disrupted attachments, and some are unaccompanied asylum seekers. Most of the children demonstrate some behavioural problems and when this is in the form of being obstructive or aggressive it can lead to their exclusion from school. An ideal mix for a group is a variety of needs and presentation of difficulties. This enables children to **find their strengths** as individuals, with compassion and understanding for their differences, along with tolerance and confidence for themselves and others.

In my role as Therapeutic Lead, I have had the good fortune to shape our methodology and the journey that young people take in an attempt to increase to the maximum the therapeutic benefits of their stay on the farm. Alongside this I have had the privilege of listening to more than two thousand children in one-to-one sessions. It is at times like this, when walking and talking, doing what I think of as therapy on the hoof, that they begin to reveal their unique hidden depths and tender-hearted parts, which previously many of them did not feel it was safe to reveal, but which often provide a key to understanding an individual's patterns and behaviours. What these children all have in common is the yearning to be understood, the desire to be loving and lovable, and most of all to be given a chance to be different, a 'better', happier version of themselves. **When behaving badly, children feel bad about themselves** and they would like this to be different. But, unlike adults who have years of embedded patterns and do not manage to change easily, the evidence of ten years of scrupulous evaluation, following up our visitors, shows that most children, when given the core conditions they need to thrive, can change train tracks and move on in a more favourable direction. Their previous negative patterns can dissolve and become redundant. They can ditch the negative labels that have weighed them down and become self-fulfilling prophecies – even if they are capable of negative behaviours, we see them with unconditional positive regard and bring out the good that exists in all of us. New ways of communication, of reflection and understanding, once within their grasp, can begin to flourish. Positive behaviour paves the way for more optimism from within the individual about themselves and about the world that surrounds them.

We have a simple programme delivered by skilful, professional, patient and energetic teams. A pre-visit to the visiting school group helps prepare them, allay their fears and increase the motivation to come to the farm. This enables our staff to become familiar with their environment, where they come from and where they return to. The selected pupils can see a film about the farm, of the environment they will be visiting, and see other teenagers enjoying the activities, rolling down hills, feeding pigs, cows and sheep, working with the horses, cooking, gardening, going off on hikes, and talking about their experience and what they got from it. It is a chance to ask questions, and voice their ambivalence and their worries; once these are aired, their anxieties are reduced. After meeting the children, we get to have a discussion with the staff who work with them, and fill in more of a picture of the individual and group needs.

One thing that is unpopular but non-negotiable: we ask them to sign a contract. The bottom line is that while they are on the farm there will be **no phones, no sweets, no smoking**, and for their safety they must work with adults in sight at all times. The children can argue their case, but the point is firm and boundaries are immovable. Clarity and consistency are at the heart of creating safety. Phones distract and divert, keeping the child from engaging fully. Sweets, fizzy drinks and food full of additives are all harmful stimulants for many children, and we find that many of those who have previously been hyperactive, by mid-week, nourished by good home cooking, now show no signs of hyperactivity. By the end of a week, the vast majority of children are glad they lived without their phones and value the boundaries we set.

Core conditions

This work has mainly happened on one of our farms, but the needs of teenagers remain the same wherever the work is done. The essential principles of our programme work in many settings. We have had the benefit of farming as a central activity and the countryside as the environment but, having worked with many of these children back in cities, we see their needs are the same, whatever the environment they happen to be in.

Underpinning all we do is an attempt to meet the core conditions for growth that Maslow described so well in his 'Hierarchy of Needs'.[6] We have to take care of their physiological needs: sleep, good food, a warm, cosy environment, attending to the physical part of teenagers' beings. We need to establish safety away from the triggers for hypervigilance[7] (for some, a cocktail of gangs, family dynamics, pressures from social media

....

6   A.H. Maslow (1962) *Towards a Psychology of Being.* Princeton, NJ: D. van Nostrand.

7   Hypervigilance means being constantly on the lookout and on the alert for danger. It renders the children fearful, anxious and untrusting of people and their environment.

and school, to mention a few). Without this, children cannot relax their defences and fully function. The environments we create for children are critical, and they need calm, nurture and support so relationships can flourish and the roots of their security can deepen. From here love and belonging can be provided, nurturing family values and a sense of community. Engaging collaboratively, in meaningful activity, can build self-esteem. Confidence seems to be the core to their thriving. Satisfaction comes from feeling that work is worthwhile and that it has outcomes which others benefit from and will recognize as a result of the stretch of hard work and effort. With all these factors in place, children can grow and develop and reach the pinnacle of 'self-actualization' that Maslow described.[8]

Relentless positivity is key to unlocking potential.

'Don't do that', 'There you go again' – for many children, the drip, drip of fault finding becomes like acid rain falling on them and corrodes their spirit to the point that they give up even trying to be good. If you are constantly told you are bad, why would you not believe it? And, if you believe it, why not prove it to others? Children who feel bad, behave badly. They will skilfully, regularly test us to confirm this. The bear trap is to oblige. We have to sidestep, be creative, divert, reroute, reframe and stay ahead of the game. Loud, noisy, attention-grabbing children need a purposeful role for this part of them. Often, if allowed to lead a group, to be a special helper rather than a nuisance, to have their strengths praised and their 'faults' under-played or at

....

8   S.A. McLeod (2018) 'Maslow's Hierarchy of Needs.' *Simply Psychology*, 21 May. Available at www.simplypsychology.org/maslow.html (accessed 07/04/2020).

best ignored, they will then become co-operative, proud rather than frustrated, successful rather than distracting.

High regard and expectations lead to better results.

As adults on the farms, we believe teenagers can work hard, collaborate in teams and have responsibilities, and that visible results can be achieved. The rhythm of the day is governed by the animals' needs, so from first thing, getting up and out, feeding the animals, the children learn that they now have dependants, and their work counts. Getting out of bed feels worthwhile, and at the end of the day of physical activity sleep is welcomed and essential for their wellbeing. Each meal is cooked and shared by a smaller group, and we sit, eat and talk. The light touch of groupwork rounds off each meal. There are check-ins and shout-outs, round the table, with everyone included, generating a concern and appreciation for each other's welfare and what they have achieved. A check-in invites the children to go round in the group and tell how they are feeling on a scale of one to ten, including variation if something made them feel, for example a nine, but something they struggled with made them feel a ten. It enables all the group to understand what kind of mood their peers are in and for us to tune in as adults to their needs. Shout-outs allow for children to be complimentary of each other, in small or larger ways, noticing the positives about a person rather than remarking on the negatives. The feedback they give is generous and kind, acknowledges the smaller deeds and larger compliments, within a culture of care. Peppered through the week they will have smaller groups to focus on the challenges they need to face, the support they need to get. Their teachers see and learn what each child wants, what help might be useful and what triggers might be destructive. Humanity is shared in the life of a farm, with fellow mud-spattered cow herders, trepidatious midwives of newborn lambs, novices at log chopping, and compatriots in the kitchen. This time, teachers and pupils occupy the same ground. Vulnerabilities and strengths mix, and deeper mutual respect grows. Teachers and pupils have undergone change.

Back at school there will be a follow-up visit of staff from the farm. Their teachers will have had the reports on how the children experienced the week, what might help back at school, and what might improve relationships at home. The children can now be each other's advocates and the isolation many children felt before coming to a farm is usually mitigated. It is acknowledged that it will not be easy, but the difference is that these children tell us they will ask for help when struggling in class and will be less likely to give up when they fear failure. These two things alone can make a world of difference. Our evaluation data (information given by each child who visits the farm) shows that children are doing far better at six weeks and six months after a visit than before the trip. Over 80 per cent of them have sustained a rise in their levels of self-esteem, and the majority of children who were at risk of exclusion are no longer at risk just six weeks on from their residential. Six months on from their visit, the statistics are even more impressive. Like small snowballs, as they roll downhill, gathering positive experiences, they will grow in confidence and small successes build further success. Come rain or shine, on the charity's farms near Monmouth, Herford, Lewes or Bath, the teenagers are there: building resilience, motivation and confidence, facing the weather, the long hikes, the hard days' farming, the challenges of living in a group and being away from the familiar.

The structure of this book

My aim in this book is to help the reader to enter the world of teenagers but also to have a road map for themselves when they feel lost, confused or confounded by the young people they live and work with. I hope you can take from it whatever is useful to your relationships with this age group.

Chapter 1 introduces the context of modern life and its pressures, how currently we have a unique cocktail of factors that impinge on the young. The world is now a larger place, through television and media brought right into our homes, and often seemingly impossible to filter. Tragedy exists and is relayed from every corner of the globe. Disturbing stories get told and retold. Information is unedited and undigested and impinges on the young. We can no longer protect the freedom of their imaginations and the golden window of childhood to experiment through play. Climate change, political instability, and racial and religious conflicts are all brought to children's doorsteps. In addition, it seems to me that that more families are struggling to keep things going and make ends meet. Often our visiting children feel that their parent or parents are under financial pressure; they often describe them as unavailable and stressed. Families in the broadest sense are where children learn their values, and the old expression 'It takes a village to raise a child' is more pertinent than ever. The teenage brain is social, and social connection is fundamental to our humanity.

Many children are growing up in families beset by anxieties, such as anxiety about putting food on the table and a roof over their heads, and about finding childcare while parents are working. Anxious parents create anxious children. Teenagers will hide this and behave in odd ways, but beneath the surface they will be struggling, finding it challenging to keep up. They too have pressure: to do well at school, to be good at home, to find firm friends and to imagine a future alongside finding a role, an identity, and often a mate. These stresses accumulate anxiety in the minds and emotions of the young and our experience is schools are worried about the increasing signs of mental health issues in teenagers, which needs to be attended to by means of greater resources.

Most teenagers are primarily focused on their peer group as they have become social creatures, but social life can feel unfiltered and is often now experienced through phones, away from adults who might mediate and help digest the impact of relationships. Phones with Instagram, Facebook and Snapchat can keep the pressures up, leave teenagers feeling transparent, under the spotlight and scrutinized at every turn. Image is paramount and projecting confidence and a cool image is the most that they can manage. Vulnerability and confusion are so often hidden. Teenagers have multiple levels of distraction to occupy their minds, but little time to focus, relax and then refresh.

For many young people the chance to play and explore, to have some unsupervised free time, has become a thing of the past. The streets feel unsafe and children's testimonies in this book describe the terrors they face. Gangs and sexual predators have become prominent in their minds. Safety, the core element to doing more than survive, for many has gone. The sense of confidence in community has been eroded in many cities, and conditions to thrive are often just not there. Hearing from the teenagers themselves, we can understand their difficulties; they provide some answers and suggest how things could change and the futures they might have.

Chapter 2 introduces the growing body of knowledge showing that the **teenage brain** is a wonderful but supercharged thing. It is developing at such a rate and its potential for growth and change is so great that it is very easy to under estimate. Whereas in the past we heard how the first three years of life were essential to the development of the child, we now know that adolescence is also a golden window of opportunity for 'upgrading' the brain.[9, 10] The behaviours of this age group are easier to make sense of if we understand how the adolescent brain develops. There is 'on the one hand a great interest in socially rewarding stimuli and increased interaction with peers but slowly developing control of emotions, rational and affective judgements on the other hand'.[11] Peers start to take precedence over parents. Taking risks is essential to learning. Being reasonable one minute, and entirely unreasonable the next, is par for the course. Teenagers can switch modes, seem unrepentant, and move on in a moment. As adults, we process more slowly, hold grudges, and want reasons. We need to work with them, not always against them, guide them and inspire

....

9   Center on the Developing Child at Harvard University (2016) '8 Things to Remember about Child Development.' Available at www.developingchild.harvard.edu/resources/8-things-remember-child-development (accessed 07/04/2020).

10 B. Hohnen, J. Gilmour and T. Murphy (2019) *The Incredible Teenage Brain*. London: Jessica Kingsley Publishers.

11 G. Scerif and K. Cohen Kadosh (2017) 'Brain Development in Teenagers.' Available at www.oxfordsparks.ox.ac.uk/content/brain-development-teenagers (accessed 07/04/2020). This article goes on to say: 'The interplay between these functions and, in brain terms, their changing "cross-talk", may explain why adolescence is characterised by a high incidence of risk-taking behaviour and high risk of developing social anxiety. It might also explain the positives: exploration, enthusiasm for new experiences. We also know that teenagers' sleeping patterns change.'

them, teach by modelling good behaviours and let them learn through their successes.

Chapter 3 focuses on adolescence with its multifarious tasks of development. This age group is psychologically caught between worlds. Adolescents simultaneously crave and fear independence from parents and family. They fear their dependency and yet yearn for it and for safety. They struggle to find their identity, their individuality, but simultaneously strive to be liked by friends and fit in. They can be agreeable in one moment and then switch to disagreeable the next. They think in broad brush strokes, can catastrophize and then suddenly recover. As adults we can feel baffled, bruised and contradicted, and along with our children feel furious and then ashamed. 'Splitting' (as described in Chapter 3) is the psychological mechanism that makes adolescents feel right. Siding with peers against parents, friends against foes, mother against father, sister against brother, they protect their vulnerabilities by seeing the world as opposed. This is their defence mechanism to avoid being overwhelmed. They are not bad, or mad; they are just living through a period of tumultuous emotions. This chapter will help explain what, psychologically, might be happening and holds a candle of hope for the future.

Chapter 4 introduces the **defence mechanisms** we all use to protect us; but when they are triggered in teenagers, they often act to confuse. Most teenagers are supersensitive. If they feel at all anxious or unsafe, their instinct is for survival, and just like an animal some may fight, some take flight, others even freeze. The fight defence in the form of aggression or defiance may be triggered by fear. The flight may be in the form of withdrawal, deflection or denial, all triggered by a feeling of being overwhelmed and the need for protection. The freeze response can be confusing as children may 'play dead'[12] with their emotions, but again the cause is most likely to be some perceived threat. When we recognize these defences and the behaviours they create, we can respond more appropriately, not as another aggressor, taking their emotions prisoner with reasoning and arguing, but helping them feel safe. As adults we tend to resort too often to lecturing and miss the first stage in communication of simple observation or just listening. We may often want to escape into our own defence mechanism of rationalization as it is uncomfortable to be alongside a child's psychic pain. I use case studies to describe some triggers that might be familiar to you, the reader, alongside children's own testimonials. This chapter will, I hope, help provide a handbrake for reflection, before we as adults, as too often happens, push things to escalate.

Chapter 5 tries to describe the key to all things: **how to communicate**. Using real stories of events and experiences, I unpack the toolbox we need to get better at connection. Stress is a modern-day virus which can infect all children and adults alike, be they teachers or pupils, parents or children. Stress then affects our concentration, our ability to listen well, to not over-react and to give good attention to one another. But children need our good attention in order to thrive. Healthy communication is at the heart of all relationships. It involves listening as well as talking, noticing and observing, and reading the clues of moods and behaviours. So often we get it wrong;

....

12 Playing dead, numbing and dumbing down emotions, is a form of self-protection and insulation to keep further stress at bay and hold the impact of others at arm's length.

we are preoccupied, jump the gun, are too agenda-driven. The angry child is often troubled, the controlling child may be anxious and driven, and the silent child is not necessarily stubborn but confused and without words. Unless we get alongside them in our understanding, we often make things worse. Building trust requires taking care. Caring means being bothered, trying to understand, being willing to be rebuffed, and not reacting to hostility, but being patient and kind. It means starting where the child is, not where we are heading. Listening trumps talking. Genuine curiosity is better than making assumptions. If we miss the key messages, we will turn off on the wrong track. Positivity is essential in so far as a child needs to feel liked. If they trust us, they will work with us, and patience will eventually win through.

I have taken many of my lessons from the 'horse's mouth' – young people who shared their honesty, their experiences and their inner realities – as well as from getting it wrong myself and finding out what works. I have tried to limit my own 'psychobabble' to communicate with the reader in a straightforward way while distilling the benefits of research and sharing the narratives of the young. Their identities have been changed to protect confidentiality, but their stories and issues are real. I hope that in reading this book, you will feel curious, hopeful, enthused, and want to develop your relationships with young people, enjoying their vitality and the challenges they set. I hope you will feel compassionate towards their struggles and the feeling that so many of them have that they are constantly walking on thin ice!

Jessica, a former visitor's testimonial

Considering my strong distaste for animals and countryside life prior to this trip, believe me when I tell you it was life-changing. When I was first offered this opportunity, I immediately pulled a face. Me? In the countryside? Pft. But looking back now, it would have been ridiculous of me to turn it down.

When I first arrived at the farm and we were asked to hand in our food and phones, I was truly sceptical of whether I would even last the week. Then it all began from there. I found myself doing things I would have entirely refused to do back in London, from cleaning out pig faeces to jumping into a freezing cold river. The entire week we woke up early to do food rounds for the farm's animals (of course, we all fought over bottle-feeding the baby sheep) before coming back in to eat breakfast that one of the groups had cooked, then heading back out to break our backs by doing something along the lines of lifting logs of wood or cleaning out a chicken pen. But the fatigue didn't stop there. Every evening we put our boots back on and went on a walk, and let me tell you, those walks were hours long and left us all moaning so much that I'm pretty sure all the members of staff secretly wanted to leave us behind in the fields. Yet, as exhausted as we all were by the end of the day, coming home was the best part. And yes, we referred to that house as our home probably by the second day in. As we sat around that iconic wooden table every night, we gave check-ins of how we were feeling and shout-outs of appreciation to somebody at the table who deserved it; and watching each person's face light up when their name was said was honestly such a pure moment of happiness. And that's exactly what I found there. Jamie's Farm had become my happy place.

...

With all the distractions going on in London, we're so lost in our own lives and our own problems that we sometimes forget to remind ourselves of all the beautiful things we need to appreciate. Having sat on those hills by myself pondering about the 101 things on my mind, looking out at such a picturesque view suddenly made it all go away. All the worries and the troubles and the stress disappeared just like that. And it was there that I realized that we spend far too much of our energy and time on the meaningless things in a busy city life, when really there are so many mesmerising things we have never experienced that we have no clue about; all the places you still haven't been, all the things you still haven't done, all the things you still haven't seen, are nothing but a mere mystery to us Londoners. This city life has blinded us from seeing that those things are what really matter. And although the majority of you reading this will probably forget all about it in two days' time, all I want is for at least just one person to take this in and understand it. Understand that this experience will change and shape you into a different person. There are terrible parts of yourself that you will leave behind there and forget that version of you ever existed. There's also going to be some amazing new parts of you that you'll bring back with you. Well, at least I know I did. As well as bringing back my newly found love for dogs, I also brought back something far more special than that: memories of the experience of a lifetime.

Jessica, age 15

CHAPTER 1

Cultural Context

'What's wrong with this generation? We were never like this!' my mother says. She feels I am over-protective of this generation, making excuses for bad behaviour; and that in the scale of hardships, life today is full of privileges that she never had. Life was hard post-war, so why is it apparently so difficult for adolescents today?

Culture has changed. For those young people who are feeling unsafe, impinged upon by social media, with a stressed, isolated family that is strapped for cash, it has changed for the worse. 'There is nowhere to play,' young Thomas says. He is 11 and wants to run, build dens, explore, kick a football in the street, climb a lamp post and more. Thomas wants some freedom, but ideally 'managed risk'. He would love to be making his own adventures with friends in the park, but he is not allowed out unsupervised. He is frustrated and lonely from the time he comes home. His mother is working, his dad has gone, and his sister is 16 but is usually at her boyfriend's house. Mum says the streets are not safe and Thomas must stay indoors, so he plays on his Xbox all evening but then cannot sleep. In the morning he is late for school and his teachers are cross, and Thomas feels a failure as in last night's virtual competition he lost.

Thomas's great-grandfather lived in this neighbourhood. He was one of six siblings and they played in the street. Football and boxing, friends down the road, building dens, Thomas's great-grandfather was never inclined to be bored. He was allowed out till 8pm and knew where he stood. His father was a disciplinarian and the rules were clear. He ate a simple diet; sugar was a treat. His mum did some work at home, sewing and mending, but the children had jobs and responsibilities to share. The house was never empty, mealtimes were regular, and all the family sat down together. They had little money but when times were rough they felt the community cared. In times of sickness the grandparents helped; there were uncles and aunties and extended family on tap.

Change is necessary and inevitable, but for Thomas and many teenagers that we know and work with the world as it is now is all they know, and for some of the more disadvantaged, it does not feel safe but full of fears. There are too many pressures and opportunities to fail; it can feel full of criticism and potential judgement. There is a lack of safe spaces, and places to congregate, which limits access to real-life friendships. At home and at school, teenagers' behaviour is often difficult, and I think that part of this is caused by cultural pressure. Parents may be struggling to stay together and money worries are rife. Childcare is frequently needed, with working parents not often home, even at night. Many children who visit the farm speak of the difficulties of their parents finding cover for themselves when they are at work.

Social media

Aspiration and inspiration are key to a child's mindset. Not all media and communication that filters into the home is damaging. Global information, discussion and debate can mean sensitive issues get aired; identity, politics, religion and the like are available for debate. Knowledge is more available, and children can be less isolated. On social media, minority groups, such as people with disabilities, may get a better chance to mix, and sexual identities are more open. But much of this awareness can be polluting if not filtered, and our children sometimes need us, as adults, to mitigate the negative influences, and direct children to more inspirational and educational material.

Phones and TV take up more time than they used to, and escaping from the media is hard to do. **Too often, the constant reminders of tragedy, mistrust, violence and crime** colour in the background of all that young people do. These things have always existed but have never been so prominently present in our consciousness. With graphic TV pictures and the plethora of news forms, all within their homes, it is hard to insulate very young children and give their imaginations unpolluted free rein. From a young age they hear on the TV repeated stories of threats to our extinction with climate change worrying young minds into catastrophic thinking. They hear of human acts of depravity, of dangers in the streets and violence in the home. Many girls in particular are speaking to us about their fear of the world being peppered with potential paedophiles. All these anxieties fill their minds with mistrust and fear — danger can be imagined at every turn. They walk past a news stand to hear someone else denigrated. At home the TV is on, with politicians arguing and accusing each other of lies; and in the news bulletins between programmes the teenagers hear about stabbings and other crimes. The media gossip is usually humiliating someone, whether in magazines or YouTube. Whereas someone previously was thought to be good, they are now disparaged, and people seem to revel in this. This exposition of failure and the **tendency to shame** are entering young people's consciousness, shaping their views and potentially eroding their trust. Many primary school children are not allowed to walk to school, and almost certainly there will be no unsupervised play. Their physical world has shrunk, with limited exploration. As **managed risks** are less accessible, their **resilience gets less opportunity to grow**. Journalists now refer to a 'snowflake generation', but it seems the media has created much of the fear, and the fear has certainly grown. When teenagers have grown up with anxiety and stress all around them, they can become hypervigilant and their emotions will flare at the slightest signal of danger. It is unsurprising that adolescents are often troubled; in school they can be difficult to teach, at home difficult to reach.

Teenagers' views on technology and social media

Social media is part of the cultural context, and to understand its impact I am turning to the teenagers for their point of view. They are the experts, and they are refreshingly honest. The picture they paint is shades of grey. It is all more complex and contradictory than we often imagine. Carmen is confidently vociferous. She says, 'It makes things more efficient, knowing what is happening, arranging to meet, seeing friends and being kept in the loop. If you have something to share, like music or blogging, there is always an audience there. Some are really rubbish but some are so cool.' Carmen makes a good point about creativity, and there certainly are audiences on tap, if you are brave and willing to 'put yourself out there'.

Jeremiah likes information. He enjoys using his phone because it gives him answers. He is a curious person and loves learning, and loves the fact that responses are so instant. I recognize that increasingly we all use the internet in this way — needing to fix something, search for directions, find restaurants, and holidays, book appointments or pay a fee — and that it saves time. But this has limitations. It is without interaction, conversation or warmth. Efficiency is clearly increased, but for those who live or work alone, is it at the expense of potential isolation?

Carmen and Tom are 14 and 16 and tell me how they stay in their rooms from the time they get home from school till nearly the next day. They say many friends are the same. For some it's due to a lack of opportunity for any other pastimes; some live in families leading disparate lives; for some it is the fear that there is a lack of safety in the outside world (for example, they live in areas with regular acts of violence, and some feel controlled by gangs). Their phones and relationships on social media have become the safer zone. The phone means they do not feel alone. It is how they 'socialize' and entertain, and without it they feel isolated. The phone is a lifeline. Sharon admits how much she likes it: 'There is less chance that you will be found to be boring, unattractive, on social media.' She feels in control of what she chooses to share and it's the side of herself she is keen to promote. 'Sometimes,' she admits, 'it is spiced up to look more interesting. The downside is, you feel you have to keep up a front, be funny and entertaining to not be found out. You can get the impression that everyone else's life is perfect. The bits that I feel rubbish about get hidden.'

Competition comes in so many forms in our culture, and measurement and comparison seem to be the norm. These young people are telling me they feel the pressure to appear to be perfect and the gap can only widen between what's inside them and what they feel prepared to share. It is all too easy to have your cover blown and shaming is rife. It is an unsettling feeling they describe of walking on thin ice. Being literate, or witty, or confident or popular — there are many ways young people feel pressured and not measuring up. And the fact that young people are often connected via their phones from the very first moment they wake up until they fall asleep means there is never a break from this pressure – even in what would in previous generations have been the private sanctuary of your bedroom.

Sharon is quite different; she is shy and has a stammer but can conceal this in her texting. She says she feels less anxious when able to use the phone. She speaks about some of her friends with physical disabilities who like the level playing field when they can use technology, join in, be smart and quick. One of her friends is in a wheelchair but loves virtual gaming and is thought of as a pro. Not only do they feel good at this but also they have a social network that would in other ways be impossible. It seems for many the plus side outweighs the negatives and it is all a question of balance.

Hector, who has been to the farm a few times, has his own views: 'Before I came to the farm, where we're not allowed phones, I thought I would miss it. I then discovered that building real physical relationships, where you see people and do things together, felt better to me than those I had on social media. I have deleted my Facebook, Instagram and Twitter accounts. I feel freer and more in the real world. I needed to have the experience of being without the phone to learn that. I wish I had found a way to limit it before. It's addictive. You stay up too late and sleep less and worry about not keeping up. **It's like having a full-time job managing your social media!**'

Boundaries and sleep

While the phone is so important and keeps teenagers in contact with each other, the downside is it can be compulsive and they struggle to regulate usage. This is where many young people tell me they need adult help. They wish their parent would set the boundaries, turn off the internet and take the phones away at a reasonable time of night. In the impulsiveness of the moment, they don't want to be without them, and find it's hard to know when to switch off. They agree they might argue the matter, but acknowledge that they need and want help, as setting boundaries on your own is sometimes just too difficult. Personally, I wish my own phone would cut off at 9pm and leave my brain free to settle before bed. While I know that I should take charge of it, to do this is another matter, as just like the teenagers, I find it hard to have sufficient resolve and be consistent and self-disciplined. Teenagers are quite honest and say they will often lack sleep, staying on their phones gaming until the early hours of the morning, then feel rubbish the next day. It is hard for them to be their own gate-keeper when in the thrall of such excitement. Simply taking technology away in the heat of the moment can cause its own disturbance. If negotiated at a good time, with clarity and clear purpose, we can help create a balance that is hard to do alone. Despite the arguments and flare-ups, teenagers want to know where they stand; they like firmness, not autocracy, and consistency without rigidity, and high expectations that come from belief in them. Stricter teachers are usually more popular as long as they are felt to be reasonable, understanding and fair. The teenager's nightmare is to have to feel responsible for the adult. They will worry and feel guilty if they think we might crumble; and if they feel they can destroy us, then they will be scared.

Detrimental effects of sleep deprivation

It seems we are only just realizing how our health at all levels is affected by lack of sleep. Most adults recognize themselves to be debilitated by lack of sleep. The days after sleepless nights can feel torturous. Our emotions feel amplified, our resources to manage and contain stress are diminished, concentration can feel compromised. The same factors affect children. Hours spent on their gaming or phones late into the night means they often have fewer hours of rest. On top of this, some researchers now argue that the blue light of phones and computers at night disrupts the brain's production of melatonin.[1] This in turn affects the circadian rhythms which we need to sleep. Once the phone or computer is switched off, the brain remains on!

....

1   C. Czeisler (2013) 'Perspective: Casting light on sleep deficiency.' *Nature 497*, S13. Available at https://doi.org/10.1038/497S13a (accessed 07/04/2020).

If teenagers are playing games on their devices, this usually involves levels of high excitation and produces adrenaline which lingers undigested in the body. Increased heart-rate and cortisol levels counter the body's attempt to relax and then fall asleep. All this affects not just how long teenagers sleep, but the quality of that sleep. To help as a parent or carer, we can maintain good connections, not let our teenagers go to bed straight after a row or under pressure that will disturb them, and help them to form good sleeping habits which will support and contain them.

There are now links made between sleep and mental health,[2] as well as physical health for all ages. Brain research is indicating that since the teenage brain is changing, growing and processing information at such a fantastic rate, teenagers need extra sleep to download things.[3] If they sleep late in the mornings at weekends and holidays, it seems this is not such a bad thing as sleep is now thought to be a wonder drug that helps general health.

Cyber bullying

Some of the young people have had sadder and more worrying experiences to share. 'Bullying on social media is too easy,' Carmen says. The teenagers tell how it can be devastating in its reach. It takes little courage as sometimes the perpetrator

....

2 K.L. Modecki and B.L. Barber (2017) 'Mobile phones in the bedroom: Trajectories of sleep habits and subsequent adolescent psychosocial development.' *Child Development 89*, 1. Available at https://srcd.onlinelibrary.wiley.com/doi/abs/10.1111/cdev.12836 (accessed 07/04/2020).

3 National Sleep Foundation (n.d.) 'Teens and sleep.' Available at www.sleepfoundation.org/articles/teens-and-sleep (accessed 07/04/2020).

can remain anonymous. There have always been people who bully. Working with children and adults who bully, it is my experience that they are usually victims themselves of emotional cruelty, be it from siblings, parents, peers or authorities. It is tangible how fearful young people are of the pervasive power of the internet and the reach of cyber bullying. As teachers, therapists, youth workers and parents, we hear of its effects. It can be extreme and persistent, and can create such despair, shame and depression that in too many cases it has culminated in young people tragically trying to take their own lives. One problem is that bullying through social media is too easy. It enables cowards to not have to face their victims, it can escalate quickly and thoughtlessly, it can attract people to join in who are projecting their own lack of self-worth. It is not just the preserve of children, so its toxicity extends. It is hard to believe the depth of cruelty and disparagement that some adults are willing to go to. Politicians are now targeted, as well as royalty, footballers, musicians and actors; anyone seems fair game for the frustrated venom that can be messaged all too easily. Girls and women get a lot of publicity but are not the only victims. Boys can get their fair share of cruelty and feel it as deeply. Sometimes as a society, I think we are less aware of their pain.

Whereas in the past people might retreat to some place of safety from bullying, now with the technology we have in our lives the corrosive messaging can get into our homes and even bedrooms. There is nowhere to hide, short of refusing to look at social media. Even when doing this, a targeted person will know that many others are seeing, and maybe believing, the stories, lies and exposures that denigrate people's lives.

Sexual exposure

Cruelty is part of human nature but that does not make it hurt less. Throughout history there have been terrible emotional and physical brutalities that have become institutionalized and sanctioned (such as the atrocities in the Auschwitz concentration camp). There is tremendous power in group culture, with the pressure to conform and the potential for absolutions of personal responsibility; and peer pressure has always meant that bullying, while appalling, has often been part of life. The degradation of women has long been used as a form of social control, but often this happens subconsciously. For example, the incidence of rape is higher in war zones.[4] There is a primitive and destructive force that can emerge in a group, with no moral compass to give guidance. Several girls have visited the farm wrapped up in their own wounds, and it has transpired that they have been victims of cruel shaming, when hidden cameras have been used to film sexual activities and then these have gone viral.

Shakira was a girl who had experienced humiliation, having been sexually exposed on social media by the young man she had thought was her boyfriend who put a film of the two of them online for all to see. She came to the farm in a depressed and introverted state. While she was awash with the toxicity of her feelings of shame and embarrassment, I realized my job was not to join the 'upset' and outrage but to be empathic and also positive, to help her feel that she was not defined by this event. As she became less withdrawn and felt supported,

....

4   I. Chang (1997) *The Rape of Nanking*. London: Penguin.

she was able to feel her anger. Anger can be energy if directed constructively. Shakira realized she was not alone, that many girls had been similarly duped, that the power of the bully only existed in the boys concerned if she became the victim. She heard of the '#MeToo' movement and began to identify with other girls and women who had suffered sexual exploitation. She came to recognize that the viral video of her said more about the degradation of the boy who posted it than it did about demeaning her.

Living within a different micro-culture at the farm, she rose to the challenge and became less withdrawn. She came out of herself and demonstrated her care for others, and with her hard work, generosity and emotional courage she was able to feel appreciated, liked and likeable again. After consultation with her teachers, a managed move to another school was agreed, which allowed Shakira to start again. She needed to feel she could shed her past. A year later I heard that she had developed her confidence and risen to the challenge of not being defined by the cruelty of others; she had also started a support group for other young women who had had similar experiences. Although Shakira had once been a victim of social media, she had taken control of it, using its positive potential to create a connection between people who had shared similar experiences. Shakira taught me all over again that it is not what happens to us that counts most but how we deal with it.

Where does this come from and what have we to learn? I have listened to young men, teenage boys, in various groups and have been amazed. Given a chance to be thoughtful and authentic, they have begun to unravel what seems to be their own feelings of powerlessness. They acknowledge the 'go to' place of bravado, the hiding in safety in numbers, but in a modern society they often feel intimidated by girls. They can easily find a scapegoat, and join a bandwagon of boys, setting out to humiliate and intimidate the girls. The world of phones and messaging, with its easy quick access, often circumnavigates their conscience. It is fed by impulsiveness and teenagers can allow things to happen; then once the situation has gone viral, it is too late.

Is there a blunting of emotional resonance and sensitivity that happens when children grow up in a world where dramatization and violence become normalized? Video games, sensationalism in the newspapers, TV drama and the like: Is it harmful? It seems we don't know for sure as the jury is still out. Each generation fears the most recent changes. In the longer term we still don't know yet what specific impact technology has. What we do know is we need to mediate; we need to be part of the teenage world to help make sense of its impact; and we need to create consistent, coherent, meaningful boundaries and limits for the long term, not short term, to be sure they are adhered to. We cannot hide our children away from modern-day culture, but we need to look at our own relationship with it, as well as theirs, and digest it together.

Social media may bring into our homes an awareness of gang culture for our children and ourselves. We hear about it not just when we are out in the street; it is in our homes with stories every day on the news on TV. It is in music and film, sometimes glamorized, sometimes denigrated, and for teenagers it presents a huge moral maze.

Gangs

One glorious autumn day working in our city farm, Joseph, a young Year 7 boy is sitting in the barn refusing to move. He looks stubborn, defiant, but underneath I wonder if he is upset and anxious. I sit down next to him and say it seems important for him not to join in right now; it is not as if he is not up to it, but too big a part of him is keeping him wanting to sit here and wait. He looks at me sideways, a bit surprised I am not trying to persuade him to go outside.

It feels more important to start from where he is rather than pushing him to join the group. 'Maybe you have had a bad day, or bad week? I am sure you have your own good reason for feeling down and not able to join the gardening group. Could you tell me a bit about what is adding up to you feeling glum?'

Joseph looks up with misery in his eyes. 'It all started,' he said, 'when I went to play football after school with my mates. There is a gang who patrol our estate. They robbed a five-year-old of his pocket money last week. They stood outside the football area where we go to play and I was too frightened to leave. I waited till 8 o'clock when they moved away; only then could I go home. I got shouted at by my mum for being late. She's grounded me. I don't want to go out anyway. They tell me and my friends we have to give them money. We cannot go anywhere anymore to kick a ball. I feel I'm locked in at home but I haven't done anything wrong. My mum is mad at me but it's not my fault. I am in trouble at school. I can't sit still. I can't concentrate. The lessons are too long. You are expected to sit in your seat for an hour and a half.' I ask Joseph if he has shared his experiences with anyone else. 'If you "snitch", they will get you. You can't tell nobody!'

Joseph has ADHD; he needs to let off steam and be able to play after school. He clearly struggles with inactivity, yet his neighbourhood has now been shut down by threats of gangs and he feels he will not be able to go out. This knocks on to schoolwork and his attitude to adults.

Tragically, Joseph is one of thousands of young children who feel their worlds are shrinking. Life outside the home is dangerous; even the journey to school can feel like running the gauntlet. No doubt his teachers are having to bear the brunt of his difficulties without even knowing what is affecting this unhappy young man.

Hypervigilance

Every day we are hearing more about the devastating loss of young lives through **knife crime**. That is the tip of an iceberg. Below this lie the huge numbers of children who do not become the statistics or headlines but who are maimed physically and/or emotionally through their involvement with gangs, either as members or victims. Below the tip of the iceberg the numbers multiply. We are hearing daily from teenagers — those who have joined gangs and those who are affected by gangs — who live in fear. For all, there is constant anxiety and danger feels near. 'I have to watch my back' is all too common a phrase. **Hypervigilance leaves children stressed** and when stressed they are reactive. Much of the behaviour that escalates in school seems to have its roots in the fact that the streets do not feel safe and fear of gang culture rules many children's lives.

Childhood as a time for play, feeling safe to explore the physical, emotional and mental world, is curtailed. Fear drives children into solitude, into their rooms at home, and this in turn makes them more dependent on social media. **Anxiety and depression are growing problems for the younger generation.**[5]

Many of the young people we see have developed a hard and threatening exterior for themselves, as a form of self-protection. Behind the mask there is usually a softer self that does not dare reveal itself.

Callum is one such child. He is failing at school and comes to the farm. His teachers are mystified by his absences; and when he is at school, he can fly off the handle and be abusive to the staff. They know him as a bright lad who is failing to engage in studies, and his 'Like I care!' attitude is exhausting his teacher. He is on the edge of being excluded. I am sitting next to Callum at lunch one day and the conversation turns to gangs. I tell him I am trying to understand the world of gangs from the perspective of teenagers, as I am sure their experience and intelligence will help us understand better. I ask Callum if I might interview him for a podcast I am doing. He is not used to having his opinion sought, or his intelligence remarked upon. He has scripted himself as outside the school system and here on the farm, with a fresh start and different reference points for success, he proves how articulate and open he can be. He is keen, not reluctant, to have his opinion sought.

We find a quiet space and the conversation begins. Callum

---

5   J. Bernstein (2016) 'The rising epidemic of anxiety in children and teens.' *Psychology Today*. Available at www.psychologytoday.com/us/blog/liking-the-child-you-love/201601/the-rising-epidemic-anxiety-in-children-and-teens (accessed 07/04/2020).

explains to me: 'My mum is doing her best, but we worry every day. How will she pay the rent? Is there enough money for food? It gets her down. I worry. She seems be on edge all the time. We argue, and never used to before Dad left. No one knows where he is. Mum says we might lose the house. She says we might end up on the street.'

Callum looks agitated and his voice is getting stronger. 'I am the oldest. I want to help.' He explains the temptation for him to join a gang. 'This way I would get paid. OK, it might mean running drugs, but I get to change things, not just sit and wait and watch my mum suffer.' He hoped this would solve his family problems. Callum explains to me that **if you are at the bottom of the pile you are like a needle in a haystack. No one notices or cares about you** and to be 'cool' you need the £200 trainers. 'If you walk down the street, wearing those trainers, people look at you and they know, they know you are somebody!' He seems to be feeling squeezed, held in a vice between fear about his mum's mental health and fear of the gang leaders and their demands. He describes being conflicted, trying to do something 'good' but joining a gang he knows is 'bad'. This conflict is like an acid burning through and eroding his self-esteem. Deep down, Callum tells me, **he feels a constant failure**. His fears create anxiety, and **anxiety means he is easily triggered into anger**. He speaks of recognizing that he is sometimes 'unreasonable' and this is more likely to be in the form of aggressive behaviour towards his teachers as school is the only place he can let off steam. I tell Callum I am impressed by his honesty, his capacity to understand what is going on. Unlike many adults who use displacement and denial to absolve them of the pain of guilt, turning to drugs or drink, or even becoming workaholics to avoid their feelings, Callum is brave, he is not in denial, and he is willing to share his life.

Callum tells me at the end of his week that he is determined not to join the gang, having had space on the farm to retreat, to reflect, to re-evaluate. Whereas once he felt in a double bind, wanting the security, the alternative 'family', the hierarchy of male role models, the sense of going somewhere, he realizes he does not believe that this needs violence or being outside the law. We speak of how he can get support with this determination, with the help of school and the new positive relationships he is forming with the teachers who have come on the trip with him. Callum is not bad and he is not weak. He recognizes he was making some wrong decisions and looking in the wrong place for support. **His motivation was to feel some belonging to something that felt powerful and had potential.** Having experienced another side of himself that is hardworking and caring, he can see another version of himself and it is this he wants to preserve.

Safety and self-respect

Many teenagers like Callum speak of **yearning to rescue their families, their reputation, their self-respect. Safety comes in numbers** and many children describe how they are **joining gangs for protection and belonging**, to aspire to powerful membership to replace a feeling of powerlessness. Successive failure can lead to them feeling that there is nothing left to lose. It is as if their lives become meaningless and society's rules are of no consequence. A gang may offer a meaningful, explicit structure of progression, kudos and status. It may also seduce and groom children to feel valued. It may offer excitement and adrenaline opportunities in real life, not just in cyber space. Real risk is seductive and compelling to many teenage boys. If you can't beat them, you can join them. Joining forces is human nature, as is **searching for a group identity**, and feeling the power of association is compelling for this age group.

Exclusion versus inclusion

For children on the edge there is a risk of single events escalating into a slide into violence. Children who do not belong to gangs regularly tell us of their need to carry knives to protect themselves. They feel the police are no longer there to act for their safety, they are there to accuse. 'Stop and search' becomes another way they feel downtrodden, treated like lesser beings, unprotected. Children being found with a knife at school will often lead to exclusion. While it was fear, the perceived need for self-defence, that drove them to carry a weapon, the consequences of 'self-protection' can be fatal. **Exclusion from school is leaving more children at the mercy of gang grooming**. They speak of being 'kicked out', and the promise of inclusion from the gangs is appealing. When they feel 'down and out', there is a strong sense of rejection and not a lot left to lose. If trying to fit into the mainstream values has failed for them and their feeling of trying to do the right thing has been defeated, the promised dividends of joining a gang can be seductive: money, protection, belonging and status. In those moments of rejection these offers from gangs trump the known risks to their morality and mortality, and as they have no other version of themselves to aspire to, joining the gang can feel as good as it gets.

Culture of kindness

Seeing teenagers engage in acts of violence can lead us to think that they are amoral, but this is just not true.

Teenagers crave role models and people they can believe in, and ideally those who have values that they can aspire to. In the day to day of urban lives many of today's teenagers have few options to turn to. If they feel they are failing at school, it is hard to believe in their teachers. If they are feeling that they are failures at home, unable to help keep their families harmonious and instead living with conflict, it is hard to aspire to be like their parents. If they feel that they are personally just not good enough, not sure of their identities, they cannot believe in themselves. Life is very confusing when you are a teenager and it is then that they most need something to believe in.

It is challenging as an adult to know how to engage, how to not alienate young people, how to build relationships and understand their thinking. If they feel that we are willing to give them our time, that we want to share in their lives and that we believe in their individuality and respect them, they will want to join in. Despite their facade of indifference, young people are thoughtful; their sensitivity and care may be hidden, but when it is safe for these qualities to emerge, they are considerate and not unkind. So often this side of them has had little chance to evidence itself. Boys, in particular, benefit from a culture of kindness, good male role models, diversity of thinking and a chance to care. Children's learning is from experience, unlike that of adults, whose preferred form is by understanding instructions.[6] Children are porous and absorbent, and **they learn best by seeing and doing**. We need to model positive cultural learning.

Values

On the farms we have a structure that facilitates creating and upholding values, but you can still do this in cities or schools if you choose values that you and your staff group or family can stick to. Kindness is clearly interpreted; positivity is harder to maintain but just as essential; generosity is a benchmark; and against these things everything can be explained.

We model **kindness** through care and consideration, and children follow suit. They look after animals and each other, including their staff and ours, and they visibly grow to like themselves when they get to do good deeds. Back at home or school these values translate easily, from making someone a cup of tea, holding the door open when someone's arms are full of books, offering a seat on the bus to a pregnant lady, to picking up the litter off the street. The list is endless and the benefits are the same. **Doing good makes you feel good**, and research backs this up.[7] Mental health and wellbeing have significant gains if teenagers perform acts of kindness each day.

....

6   B. Hohnen, J. Gilmour and T. Murphy (2019) *The Incredible Teenage Brain*. London: Jessica Kingsley Publishers.

7   For example, M. Wenner (2007) 'Doing good makes you feel good.' Live Science. Available at www.livescience.com/4443-study-good-feel-good.html (accessed 07/04/2020).

Positivity is about where we place our attention, whether we believe in things and hope to dream. Our **high expectations** of children are important. So often, **teenagers feel that society has given up on them and has no faith in them; that they have nothing left to lose**. If they are at a developmental stage where emotions overtake them, our faith and resilience matter even more. It is so important not to join in their negativity and get dragged down together. In spite of the invitations to descend into arguing, it is vital we hold fast, refuse the invitation and remain committed to the idea that things can be different.

Collaboration: Teenage brains are wired for social learning, and at schools and at home we need to make use of this capacity. Collaboration feeds the **need for belonging**; together, when more can be accomplished than individually, the satisfaction of achievement can be shared. Through interest and friendship groups, teenagers' **motivation will be activated**, and it is here and in teamwork alongside adults that a social creed can be forged. It provides a compass to steer them and weather their storms. Whether it be in families, schools or social areas, we need to think carefully about the culture we create and the values we adhere to; we need to involve young people in our thinking and give them inspiration to emulate.

Gangs and social media have created a **climate of moral complexity** that is possibly **more difficult to navigate** than ever before. In early childhood our children could be 'controlled'; they physically depended on us and had more need of adults. Their minds were more straightforwardly motivated by individual gain or pain. However, teenagers are at risk as their morality is defined by other people, and this leaves them very vulnerable. Our adult brain can process complex thinking, abstract reasoning and living by ethical values, but the areas of the brain that perform these functions are not thought to develop until the later teenage years or early adulthood.[8] The following chapter will look at the ways the teenage brain is changing and how we need to adapt to meet its needs. The more recent knowledge and insights from neuroscience reveal that socializing becomes the top priority in most teenagers, and emotions take precedence over logic;[9] these patterns all help us understand how vulnerable and susceptible to coercion young people can be.

....

8   S.B. Heyes (n.d.) 'Mapping the adolescent mind: How brain development and mental health interact.' Available at www.birmingham.ac.uk/research/perspective/ mapping-adolescent-mind.aspx (accessed 07/04/2020).

9   S-J. Blakemore (2012) 'Development of the social brain in adolescence.' *Journal of the Royal Society of Medicine 105*, 116.

CHAPTER 2

The Trials and Tribulations of the Teenager's Brain

Jason is shouting at his teacher, refusing to join the activity. He is red faced, pacing up and down, fists clenched, and looks ready to blow. Helen has seen Jason like this before; she calmly stands her ground, and does not raise her voice. She repeats that she would like him to come and join the group, but she can see he might need some time and suggests it would be helpful if he could pick up the coat on the other side of the yard that someone has dropped. Jason goes off, stomping, head down, muttering, arms occasionally flailing. Helen turns her attention to the group and lets them know what they will be doing, reassures them that Jason will be OK, but explains that he needs some space and that heckling will not be helpful, to her or him. She remarks that she really appreciates how patient they are being. The group have turned their attention to what they are doing next. A few minutes later, Jason returns, looking a bit down at heel, to Helen's smiling face, to her 'thank you' for his being so helpful, which she particularly appreciates as she is feeling a bit stiff today. She remarks that his reputation for being kind and helpful had been mentioned by another member of staff that morning. She turns to walk to join the group and as an aside lightly says, 'Maybe if you feel able, you might tell me later what upset you earlier.'

Within five minutes Jason is unrecognizable: engaged, smiling, calm and eager to get on. His behaviour is not uncommon for a 14-year-old boy, flipping from one mood to another, and showing no awareness of the debris he might have left in his wake. Fortunately, Helen is an experienced teacher. She does not take things personally. She knows that whatever is upsetting Jason in this moment is totally preoccupying, and his logic is very black and white. His temper needs to run its course; the adrenaline will eventually leave his system, even more quickly if he has a physical activity which will help digest this overload. He is likely to feel emotionally exhausted but want to put it behind him. Now is not the time to challenge him; he may be more reflective later.

Jason's ability to go from one extreme mood to another is not uncommon in a teenager. Helen does not bear a grudge. She has not tried to lecture him or talk about the effect of his mood on others, or his need to control his temper, or how unacceptable it is to kick off like that. She knows that later when he is not flooded with adrenaline, feeling ashamed and defensive, she might be able to have a more reflective conversation with him. Most importantly, she would like him to tell her what upset him and triggered his rage. Helen knows that Jason's flight or fight defences are raw, and he can quickly feel unsafe and then blow. He often misreads other people, misinterprets and then over-reacts. He cannot 'think logically' when churning with emotion. If she became hostile or incensed, he would react similarly. She has to model calm, thoughtful, positive behaviour.

Helen is an experienced teacher, but also curious. When we share a moment later on, thinking about Jason, we are reminded of how the new understanding coming from scientists studying the brain is helping to explain some of the things we observe in teenagers that previously seemed baffling.[1] Why are they so moody? How do they blow so hot and cold? Why do they see the world in such black-and-white terms? Why are they so desperate for peer approval? What are they thinking when they are so irresponsible and dangerous at times? Why do they get so manic, take ridiculous risks? How can they best learn? What do they need from us as adults?

For many years, the common theory was that the first three years of life were critical and damage or deficit in this period might be irreversible. This has more recently been reduced to the first six months of life.[2] Neuroscientists were, and still are, saying that indeed so much is learnt in these years (0–3 years). The rate of development of the brain is rapid and certain parts of the brain need mirroring, reflecting our enjoyment of the infant and their being. This applies particularly to infants under 6 months, but importantly in toddler years when so much learning is taking place in the first 3 years. The baby's world becomes known to it through the mother or the caregiver

....

1   M.D. Leiberman (2012) 'Education and the social brain.' *Trends in Neuroscience Education 1*, 1, 3–9.

2   Centre for Educational Neuroscience (n.d.) 'Most learning happens in the first 3 years.' Available at www.educationalneuroscience.org.uk/resources/neuromyth-or-neurofact/most-learning-happens-in-the-first-3-years (accessed 07/04/2020).

and they search for eye contact for reassurance. The mother's concern and ability to read the infant is shown in her face. Tuning into the baby's needs, interpreting its different cries, are all part of soothing and bringing a harmonizing effect to the relationship, when the caregiver can recognize the needs of the child and is able to calm and change their emotional state.

A project led in 2012 by Nathan Fox, a child development researcher, looked into the long-term neurological effects of deprivation in children born into neglect.[3] His team examined whether early neglect could be seen within brain scans many years later. They noted that: 'Institutionalised children had delays in cognitive function, motor development and language and showed deficits in socio-emotional behaviours and experienced more psychiatric disorders. They also showed changes in the patterns of their EEG [the electrical activity within the brain].' His study and others[4] pointed out that institutionalization could lead to arrested development.

Many people thought this might be permanent damage.[5] In some cases, the brain scans were devastating in revealing how little the prefrontal cortex – the area of the brain responsible for

....

3   N.A. Fox (2012) *The Effects of Early Adverse Experiences on Development: Lessons from the Bucharest Early Intervention Study*. Department of Human Development, University of Maryland. Available at www.researchconnections.org/files/childcare/pdf/Fox_Nathan_StressMtg2012.pdf (accessed 08/04/2020).

4   See D. Karas (2017) 'The connections between early institutionalization and brain development.' BOLD (Blog on Learning and Development). Available at https://bold.expert/the-connections-between-early-institutionalization-and-brain-development (accessed 13/07/2020).

5   Essays, UK. (2018) 'Effects of deprivation on child development.' Available at www.ukessays.com/essays/education/effects-of-deprivation-in-childhood-education-essay.php (accessed 07/04/2020).

planning cognitive behaviour and regulating primal emotion – had grown.[6] The news was shocking and sent ripples through the world of child development, reinforcing the importance of early experiences. There was an understandable fear that missing the golden window of opportunity in early life would lead to permanent, irreversible damage.

Thankfully this seems not to be the case. Now with the aid of the observations mapping brains of teenagers and seeing the changes as they happen, rather than studying from autopsy, or making associations from animal behaviours, we are learning that adolescence is a massive period of change and development.[7] New technologies such as functional magnetic resonance imaging allow us to observe brain functioning as it happens.

More recent studies[8] are revealing that the **brain keeps growing and developing**; indeed during adolescence there is massive change in activity **in structure and function**, and despite earlier experiences, this is a **window of opportunity**. Personality is still forming, growing and also 'pruning' (cutting back to allow space for more fresh growth). Adolescence is now often referred to as the new 0–3, and interventions and opportunities are critical

....

6   B.D. Perry and M.R.D. Pollard (1997) 'Altered brain development following global neglect in early childhood.' Society for Neuroscience: Proceedings from Annual Meeting, New Orleans. Available at www.researchgate.net/publication/260387981_Altered_Brain_Development_following_Global_Neglect_in_Early_Childhood (accessed 07/04/2020).

7   S.B. Heyes (n.d.) 'Mapping the adolescent mind: How brain development and mental health interact.' Available at www.birmingham.ac.uk/research/perspective/mapping-adolescent-mind.aspx (accessed 07/04/2020).

8   Newport Academy (2018) 'The facts about teen brain development.' Available at www.newportacademy.com/resources/mental-health/teen-brain-development (accessed 07/04/2020).

in this phase if we want to maximize the chance to help teenagers learn. Learning takes many forms, from being able to regulate and understand their emotions, to navigating social situations. It might be how to absorb formal school-based learning or develop practical skills; learning how to pick themselves up after failure or disappointment; or how to navigate social engagement. All these forms of brain function are interconnected and so in our approach to working and living with this age group, we need to be sensitive to all these issues. If we fail to help negotiate emotions, we will be unable to teach fact-based skills as the attention will not be there. If we ignore the child's social focus, their attention is likely to be elsewhere. We need to understand that the different parts of the brain are exerting different pressures from those of adults; if we can stay alert to this, we have a better chance of building positive relationships.

It is not until around the age of 18 that there is more organization of the neural pathways, and less susceptibility to the instinct drives that preclude logic. One of the things we need to remember as adults is that adolescents' brains are not fully developed and we have learnt from images of the brain in action that teenagers' actions are determined more by the emotional and reactive amygdala than adults whose more developed brain has a greater use of the logical frontal cortex.[9] This is not fully developed in many until they are in their twenties. It may be that much of our purposeful reasoning and talking to young children, asking them to be responsible for moral choices,

9   American Academy of Child & Adolescent Psychiatry (2016) 'Teen Brain: Behaviour, Problem Solving, and Decision Making.' Available at https://www.aacap.org/ AACAP/Families_and_Youth/Facts_for_Families/FFF-Guide/The-Teen-Brain-Behavior-Problem-Solving-and-Decision-Making-095.aspx (accessed 18/06/20).

is falling on deaf ears. I sometimes shudder to think of how much understanding of their emotions I expected with my own children, when what they probably wanted was empathy and understanding, and a good dose of clarity and clear boundaries.

Like all new knowledge, this information is changing and growing daily. What we know is only part of the jigsaw, with a great many different influences, and no two children are alike since as humans we are affected by our culture, **environment and genetics**. We are all individuals with different factors affecting our learning and development, and, thankfully, we will probably never be able to entirely reduce our understanding to empirical science. What we do have, however, is a better understanding of behaviour that is influenced by brain changes and developments, and where the focus of activity is for many of our teenagers. In the cases of exceptions, such as **neurodiversity**, we are gaining a better sense of what likely pattern of brain function affects children with specific learning difficulties (particularly ASD, dyslexia and ADHD). Any understanding has to be flexible. Often our theories about differences can become predetermining, and experience on the farms shows that all children visiting are **more, rather than less**, capable than expected, regardless of the diagnosis or prior assessment of their abilities. Expectations at their worst can create limitations.

Cocktail of forces

Neuroscience has revealed that **huge changes are happening** at a rapid rate in the brains of adolescents.[10] This means they

---

10   B. Hohnen, J. Gilmour and T. Murphy (2019) *The Incredible Teenage Brain*. London: Jessica Kingsley Publishers.

are unpredictable, supersensitive, and learning new things daily. Yes, they do seem more susceptible to stress and to feeling emotions powerfully. At times they find it hard to reason or to think 'logically'.[11] There is increasing evidence that this is exacerbated by physiological changes and the reconfiguring of brain and hormonal changes. In addition, there are the psychological stresses of growing towards independence and ambivalence towards separation from parents. Alongside all this is the dependency on peer approval and the search for identity. It is a huge amount to process, especially when accompanied by a climate of constant fear of failure.

Adolescence is a period when emotions are hard to manage, and adolescents are vulnerable to mental health problems such as depression, self-harming, eating disorders and anxiety. UK statistics show that teenagers are three times more likely to experience **mental health problems** than young children.[12] Young Minds statistics[13] from Margot Sunderland show that 1 in 6 young people between 16 and 24 have symptoms of a mental disorder and shockingly that in 2017 suicide was the most common cause of death for both boys and girls in this age range. Mental health is a big issue that we cannot sweep

....

11   American Academy of Child & Adolescent Psychiatry (2016) 'Teen Brain: Behaviour, Problem Solving, and Decision Making.' Available at https://www.aacap.org/AACAP/Families_and_Youth/Facts_for_Families/FFF-Guide/The-Teen-Brain-Behavior-Problem-Solving-and-Decision-Making-095.aspx (accessed 18/06/20).

12   Mental Health Foundation (n.d.) 'Mental health statistics: Children and young people.' Available at www.mentalhealth.org.uk/statistics/mental-health-statistics-children-and-young-people (accessed 07/04/2020).

13   Young Minds (2018b) 'YoungMinds Trusts, Annual Reports and Accounts, Year ended 31 March 2018.' Available at https://youngminds.org.uk/media/2757/youngminds-annual-report-2017-18.pdf (accessed 18/06/20).

under the carpet. As adults we need to acknowledge when young people are struggling, be able to listen and talk to them with sensitivity and assist them in getting professional help. Teenagers whose emotions are affecting them to the point of diverting their thinking, living and learning will need help to understand these processes. Yet, as this is a period of such rapid change, difficulties can be helped with the right interventions at this stage. Adolescents are open to changing patterns and trying out new ways of being, and we need to explore the ingredients of what is helpful and life-changing at this crucial stage.

The potential of the adolescent brain

The joy of teenagers seems to be that they can embrace new and different experiences, despite natural cautiousness and occasional awkwardness. Young people coming to the farms have taught us that few of them have previously shown their potential. They seem to flourish with fresh starts and new opportunities. They respond enthusiastically to a rural environment, frequently remarking on the beauty and the calm. With a combination **of nurture and recognition**, a sense of purpose working together, collaborating, they gain the chance to flourish and display their talents. **Confidence** seems at the base of all things and we are always working to enhance this. Just like athletes learn best with **positive reinforcement** of the skills they do well, children demonstrate how they need encouraging feedback to enhance the likelihood that they will choose to repeat positive behaviours. A common remark from visiting adults, social workers and teachers who have prior experience of the children, is 'I don't recognize this child!' Lurking close to the surface there has often been a loving, competent teenager, previously hidden by their particularly protective masks. How can so much change in a few days? Well, it seems the **plasticity** of the teenage brain has a lot to do with this; and working with the whole child — mind, body and spirit — they gain a new sense of self that gets embedded in **experience**. An experience that involves working and living together with others creates its own narrative, and memories are encapsulated in those narratives.

Environmental effects of the brain

Nature and wellbeing

When children feel safe, their hypervigilance, which creates a flight or fight response and the production of cortisol, can rest. Ecotherapists have hypothesized that the brain's 'command centre' can turn its volume down and pause.[14] When in optimal settings rather than on alert and just trying to survive, stress and anxiety seem to decrease. Research has shown that children's brain activity changes in different environments and that in woodland settings they are more capable of learning more complex tasks.[15] The Department of Health has acknowledged that woodland and forests are Nature's Health Service.

....

14 See Mind (2020). Available at www.mind.org.uk/information-support/tips-for-everyday-living/nature-and-mental-health/about-ecotherapy-programmes (accessed 07/04/2020). The Centre for Ecotherapy provides support for vulnerable people in the local community, aiming to improve and maintain wellbeing through the use of nature-based and horticultural therapies, mindfulness and practical activities.

15 Forest Research (2003–2005) 'Forest schools: Impact on young children in England and Wales.' Available at www.forestresearch.gov.uk/research/forest-schools-impact-on-young-children-in-england-and-wales (accessed 07/04/2020).

The Wanless Report[16] reported that wellbeing needed a new approach and outlined the benefits of being in nature, with both opportunities for physical activities and also an increased sense of mental wellbeing. They stress the importance of green spaces within cities, and encourage city planners to be mindful of creating oases of calm.

People and place

The environment may not be rural but some of the qualities can be replicated. Children need a sense of continuity and feeling that some things last. Starting in the physical world is the place to create groundedness and too often we fail to recognize how our bodies affect our minds. If teenage minds are constantly shifting in their perceptions, all the more reason for us to create environments of stability. Connecting children to the physical environment and enabling them to care for it can stabilize their feeling that everything is transitory. In a classroom or on our farm there are things to take care of; and if we involve the teenagers in this physical care, it helps restore their sense of order. As mentioned above, doing a good job, a good deed, something for others, can enhance a person's wellbeing, and opportunities like this are often forfeited. Children benefit from the evidence that they did something worthwhile and good, so the feedback loop needs to be tangible, comprehensible and preferably immediate.

Our working practice will be evidenced in structures and activities and this needs to reflect stability, a sense of order

....

16   D. Wanless (2002) *Securing Our Future Health: Taking a Long-Term View. Final Report.* London: The Public Enquiry Unit.

and calm. A programme of learning or therapeutic intent, benefits from having clear boundaries and expectations for this age group. As adults we need to embody nurture and strength so the adolescent can feel we can 'hold' the force of their emotions. In order for the brain functioning to thrive, it needs stability in its psychological and social environment.

A few years ago, I visited a social project that is no longer running. The sound of children shrieking greeted me at the door, which was opened by a young woman looking harassed and anxious as a child tore past us and ran up the stairs. This after-school provision provided rooms full of choices, activities and equipment, and well-intentioned helpers. The dining room, to which I was taken for a coffee and a catch-up, was full of clattering noises and I felt the world revolving round me as the children ran around. Some were shouting and quarrelling, some were laughing hysterically, some were looking lost and confused, and I wondered who was containing them. In the midst, the odd teenager looked disgruntled and abandoned.

It transpired that the children had free range of this house and that it was thought to be good after-school care for those who had no one at home. What was missing was order, a sense of calm and of boundaries, of purposeful activity and structure to hold this. Instead, the chaotic environment reflected the chaos of their minds and homes alike. Children's brains are easily overloaded and this noise and confusion surrounding them was producing the opposite effect of what was intended, which was therapeutic after-school care. The children could not create this for themselves; they were overwhelmed by choices and the freedom was bewildering. As adults we need to craft the environment, be creative but at the same time careful and not overfill the psychological spaces of the young people's minds as their filing systems get overwhelmed and the result can be damaging.

Teenagers learn from what we do, not what we say

We learn by imitation, and seeing is believing in a teenager's world. If the adults are stressed or anxious, the children in turn become stressed or anxious. The brain is wired to notice danger and if adults are signalling all is not well, their dependants, like all young animals, get prepared to take flight from danger. Teenagers' sensors are particularly alert; they are reading our body language without us necessarily knowing it. Because their brains have become more socially curious, their antennae are primed. Sadly, this makes them particularly vulnerable to over-reacting or even misinterpreting, but the bottom line is they are looking out for danger, whatever form it takes. Our moods as adults affect them greatly and all children are typically porous; they absorb our discontent as if by osmosis and in turn can become contaminated. Stress is toxic and as adults, where we possibly can we need to support each other and take care to attend to our own difficulties, before we pass it on. And, if our strains are unavoidable, they are better honestly owned than deflected or denied, as reality is more palatable to teenagers than any form of cover-up. They struggle with lies, in any shape or form; as part of learning how to navigate their lives, in preparation for adulthood, they need to be able to read a road map that is not full of false diversions. Trust is built on honesty and emotional honesty is the foundation stone for security.

When stressed or irritated, it is hard to see or even envisage different ways of being. The old adage 'Do what I say' needs to be replaced with 'Do what I do'. **Modelling that is positive**, collaborative, thoughtful and emotionally sympathetic is more likely to produce these qualities in teenagers. Our experience at the farm is that those who visit us are often yearning to be kinder, more thoughtful, collaborative and loving. Given the chance, and within a culture where this is both expected and embodied by the adults, they take it on with far less resistance than their teachers or we ourselves would imagine. The feedback loop of positive change feeds adults and young people alike. On our own, as individuals, it can be very difficult to effect such lasting change. Working as a team, living in a community, in a family, makes a world of difference as we are experiencing, modelling, engaging in the whole of the child's perceptual, physical, emotional and developmental self. Teenagers' brains are wired to be social in their learning, finding themselves a sense of place, where they fit, who they would like to be like, and understanding relationships. They learn through role modelling with a sense of place in the 'tribe'. The positive cycle of learning involves doing, to get the sense of achievement and motivation to try again; success builds on success and they want to do things well again. If we can use the peer group in the learning, to be offering positive feedback, the learning becomes collaborative as well as individual.

Labelling and reinforcing negative patterns

So often, **inadvertently, we are reinforcing negative behaviour**. I have heard myself labelling my own children or grandchild:

'He is the boisterous one, she is the drama queen, he is the academic one...' Teachers have their versions of a child's abilities. 'Greg is so helpful, Ayesha is a nuisance, Meg is a quick learner, Sam is quite dull, Abdul never listens, Cameron is a "bad" lad, Emily is just slow.' All these labels can do much more damage than we would like to admit. If a child believes the version of themselves as a poor learner, or disobedient, they are more likely to act up to this than change our perceptions. Personally, if I feel stupid, I begin to be stupid. Even as an adult, once I know I have got something wrong and then add shame to that knowledge, my further attempts (whatever it is I am trying to achieve, such as fill in a form, learn a new skill or understand some instructions) all seem to lead to more slip-ups and mistakes and reinforce the feeling of being stupid. Many children revolve around this circle of failure. Moreover, they are tuned into any signals or communication by our faces or our actions that might show our mistrust in their ability, thereby reinforcing their own. Their brains are supersensitive to criticism and on the lookout for any evidence of our doubting them, and since teenagers are wired to notice 'judgements', any confirmation of our negativity can leave them feeling like giving up. Behind feigning indifference, finding distractions, resenting the world and disliking themselves, they can all too easily feel a failure.

Labels confer expectations and expectations reinforce patterns; children can feel confined and defined. Patterns form as adaptations, but labels are applied often as shorthand descriptors; rather than enhancing, they can limit our understanding. It may be a child is reacting and responding to their particular circumstances, which are themselves time limited. Adjustment to the needs of these circumstances and situations, with family, the school community, the classroom, the peer group and group dynamics, is often systemic. The child is part of a jigsaw, a part of a pattern that needs completing; they may form identities and behaviours to conform to other people's needs rather than to develop their own potential. Reinforcement of negative expectations seems to keep them stuck. A new beginning, a fresh start, often reveals that children are nothing like the label they carry. Labels can become a strait jacket and do the opposite to developing potential.

Risk and resilience

That car that drove past last night with teenagers at the wheel dancing with death, their own and others' lives put at risk. How could they! Are they mad, or just bad?! It seems they may be neither, but teenagers, especially boys, are more likely to want to take risks and this is not just peer pressure, gender roles, but the way their brains are developing. Risk is critical to learning. Risk, fed by the high of adrenaline, helps them define the possible and impossible. Dangers are increased if there is use of drugs and alcohol, as the teenage brain is more susceptible than the adult brain to these stimulants.[17]

As adults, we tend to use our fully developed prefrontal cortex – the bit of the brain that orders and understands what is happening. Teenagers, on the other hand, are functioning more often from the amygdala – the part of the brain that is

....

17   R. Taite (2015) 'The teenage brain on drugs.' *Psychology Today.* Available at www. psychologytoday.com/gb/blog/ending-addiction-good/201502/the-teenage-brain-drugs (accessed 07/04/2020).

often described as more linked to our reptilian brain: as in a baby, governing instinct rather than understanding or thinking. More than this, they seem to need more risk in order to develop. Without risk we do not try new things, without risk we do not understand what works and doesn't work, without risk the human race would not have developed. **Without risk we struggle to build resilience**, and resilience is thought to be key to successful futures.[18]

Our society is becoming more risk averse. Urban life for many adolescents (stuck at home, living often with many physical constraints of lack of safe spaces to socialize and play) can lead to teenagers creating their own dangerous sports, or even joining the subversive subcultures of gangs. There is talk in the media of the 'snowflake generation', insinuating that growing up in too nannying an environment may mean fewer chances to develop resilience. Some researchers are relating the increase of depression to the lack of opportunities for this generation to be exposed to managed risk through which they grow and learn.

Risk brings its own rewards. It seems that when we take risks, we produce a brain chemical called dopamine which activates feelings of excitement, thrill and pleasure. Researchers have seen that when dopamine levels are low, people can become lethargic and uncurious.[19] Dopamine is clearly good for us at the right levels, that is, having enough but not too much

....

18 Reachout.com (n.d.) 'Wellbeing and resilience.' Available at https://schools. au.reachout.com/articles/wellbeing-and-resilience (accessed 07/04/2020).

19 TrackMyStack (n.d.) '6 Symptoms of Low Dopamine.' Available at https:// trackmystack.com/articles/6-symptoms-low-dopamine (accessed 18/06/2020).

in our system. Risk becomes its own motivator as it often leaves teenagers on a high. Most teenagers are desperate for peer approval, to be liked, and to belong; they crave being part of the 'popular' group, and more than that, they seek status. Risks can be institutionalized in subcultures as tests for approval ratings. To be seen to be brave, even reckless, amidst adolescent peers can seem 'cool'. If we add in the potential effects of having taken drugs or alcohol and evidence that teenagers take bigger risks in front of their peers, risk taking can be disastrous.

Cannabis

I am reminded of Jamal. He arrived at the farm with a group of ten other boys from what was then called a 'Pupil Referral Unit', and is now called 'Alternative Provision'. He had been excluded from school and in this smaller unit he was struggling to find his level. He was tall and lanky but not very strong. Jeans hanging virtually off his bottom, he wandered around and found it hard to commit to activities. He seemed to be in a daze. Talking to his teachers, I learnt that he had used cannabis from an early age, growing up in a family that moved to new houses regularly with a mum who was struggling. The teachers shared with us that there was concern that the long-term use of cannabis had damaged his memory and concentration. He suffered from depression and panic attacks.

Jamal was with the group on a walk and they were enjoying kicking and throwing a rugby ball as we went along the bottom meadow. It was January and there had been heavy rain that had frozen over the areas of standing waters in the field. While we take the children out for a walk every day, we are always mindful of teaching them the crucial rules of the Countryside Code: especially how to enjoy the beauty of the natural environment, without putting yourself at risk.

One of the boys accidentally kicked the ball into a neighbouring field that was clearly signposted 'Keep Out', and there were several young bulls grazing around a feeder with their feet deep in mud and slurry where they had broken through the ice. Before we could blink, Jamal clambered over the barbed wire fence, ripping his clothes, and tore after the ball that had landed at the feet of a large, very startled bull. I was horrified by the speed and lack of care that took Jamal into danger. By sheer chance the ball bounced against the metal rim of the feeder and Jamal ran and collected it, before the bulls, who had scattered, even noticed. Laughing and triumphant, Jamal ran back to the fence where we had to haul him over, taking as much care as we could not to further rip his clothes or let him inflict damage on himself. His group, taken by surprise, were hysterically shouting, 'What were you thinking, Jamal?!' Their hysteria was fed by fear as they could see he could so easily have been knocked to the ground by one of the large, startled animals. The teachers were stunned, and, in our shock, we were shouting, berating him for doing something so dangerous, shouting that it was very unsafe to enter that neighbour's field. Could he not see it said, 'Keep Out'? How could he be so stupid?! Suddenly the ball slipped from Jamal's cold, muddy hands and he kicked it high back into the bulls' field and again climbed the fence and ran to retrieve it. This time he fell into the freezing boggy puddles, only just clambering out in time and returning to the fence before a group of snorting animals trampled around or potentially even over him. Jamal was pulled to safety and the group were astonished, laughing at him, shouting at him, and telling him he was mad!

I walked back through the upper fields to the farm on my own with Jamal, a soaking wet, freezing cold boy. I realized he could not be reasoned with. He was in shock, and I was too. My fear had provoked my fury and I needed to calm down and try to imagine what would have triggered his astonishing impulsive and dangerous actions. We walked mostly in silence with only my comments occasionally that I would get him some warm, dry clothes and then we might think what to do next. While he was changing, my own adrenaline was abating. Jamal had taught me a profound lesson not to underestimate an adolescent's impulsivity and need for peer approval. I felt suddenly very sad for this desperate boy who could not find an appropriate way of joining in. He had lost a good grip on reality with his drug taking and had distorted his sense of self-preservation. He suddenly seemed very small and vulnerable and he had demonstrated how at times this age group still act on impulse with little control from the part of the brain that governs logic! Here was a teenager with a toddler's impulsivity and lack of self-control, but a teenager now driven by a need for peer approval and love of risk taking. Like so many young men he lacked a handbrake to stop his instincts for action running away with him.

I was reminded how sensible decision making does not start significantly increasing until around the age of 17 and that prior to this, due to the lack of maturation of the frontal lobes where a lot of thinking takes place, younger teenagers have not matured enough to regulate messages from other parts of the brain. They can be in the grip of their impulsivity and emotions.

Towards the end of his five-day stay I caught up with Jason. I asked him how his stay was going, aware a lot had happened since I witnessed his first 'tantrum'. At first, Jason said, he thought it was 'shit' on the farm. He had hated the mud, the smells, the hard physical work, going out in the rain, the cold and wind. After a while, he said that he relaxed, and stopped watching his back, began to enjoy the different challenges of long walks, working with large animals, rounding up sheep, making new friends, beginning to trust adults, all with their own risk of being new and different. The reward was that he could feel good about himself as his peers gave him honest, heartfelt feedback. They appreciated the small and real things about him. He said he had not felt likeable before and he knew that his association with a gang meant he was at risk of being involved in violence. He now knew that was not how he wanted to be. He had an alternative. He could use his courage to show leadership, to engage in hard physical work, to show consideration and kindness, all qualities he knew he possessed but had not previously translated into his context at school and at home. Now he felt some aspiration to take these qualities on to college, to train, to find a profession. He said he would like to be a plumber and he now believed he could be a success, not a failure.

Jason reminds me of how we need to feel needed, need to feel effective and need to feel that people notice. His teacher Gareth's version of him when he came to the farm was that this was a last chance. He was on the edge of exclusion. He was dragging his past misdemeanours around with him and was labelled 'a problem'. Gareth felt there was more to Jason but was frustrated. In the school environment, he could see Jason felt lost in the crowds and unable to stand out for anything positive; he was slipping into despondency. Gareth said his conversations with Jason usually ended with 'What's the point! It's a waste of time. People think I am a waste of space!!' He was failing to turn up for school. Gareth wanted to give him a last chance and was amazed when he was working with Jason doing physical jobs to see his commitment, his strength, his determination. Success built success. Learning was achieved through a positive feedback cycle. Gareth commented on how he needed to take this back to the classroom as a Geography teacher, and find a reward cycle that could build new confidence but also those new brain connections!

How to help rather than hinder

Much of what we know of what works or doesn't work in relating to, teaching, working with and supporting teenagers comes from common sense, experience, observation and intuitive understanding. Some of the new research does, however, highlight that we cannot treat teenagers only as if they are mini grown-ups.[20] Apart from their individual differences, and need to be understood as unique, they are struggling with a massive period of shifting change, internally and externally.

Philippa Perry, in her book *The Book You Wish Your Parents Had Read*,[21] urges parents to be empathic with their teenagers

....

20   R. Dahl (2004) 'Adolescent brain development: A period of vulnerabilities and opportunities.' *Annals of New York Academy of Science* s1021, 1–22.

21   P. Perry (2019) *The Book You Wish Your Parents Had Read.* London: Penguin Life.

and try to see how they are framing the world in that snapshot of time. She writes (p.226):

> The teenage brain can have moments as powerful as that of an untamed wild animal. And although it might be difficult for you to keep being empathetic with this at times, keep trying. And be optimistic: their frontal lobes will catch up.

She reminds us of how hard life can be as a teenager still trying to find your place in life; attended by so much fear felt in places of insecurity, teenagers are vulnerable to the trigger of the flight or fight reactions. Perry (p.227) reminds us that developmentally '[w]e are at our worst just before we conquer the next hurdle in our life'.

Adults are not another species, and we see how at times of stress, anxiety or overwhelm we resort to many of the behaviours of our teenage self. The children at Jamie's Farm have taught me to be more patient, more curious and less judgemental. Messing up is part of learning and moving on. Fresh starts and optimism seem vital.

In terms of behaviour, some behavioural policies, such as zero tolerance, or one strike and you are out, are going to penalize adolescents with their more impulse-driven behaviours. This tragically leaves them on the outside of the mainstream and often progressing down a route towards gang involvement, crime and antisocial behaviours. Once they feel bad, they become really bad, with nothing to lose, living in the moment with undeveloped logical brains. Maybe we expect too much at a point when adolescents need maximum support.

Teenagers are passing through a critical phase, and the

psychology of their development is now better understood. The next chapter examines how hard they are working internally and developmentally to work though critical psychological developmental phases. This information can only help us to be better at relating, and in turn inform our relationships, helping this age group navigate their last stage of childhood before independence and adulthood. They need us to give them some space and credit, but not stand too far back, as it is in tandem with adults, and as part of communities, that children will best thrive and find a moral compass.

CHAPTER 3

Stepping Through the Changes – Adolescent Development

Karl and Jazz

Karl is a lanky lad. His long hair lies at 45 degrees across his face, giving his head a permanent tilt as he looks out from behind the curtain of hair. He is smooth-skinned and looks young in the face for a boy of 14; here are no signs of facial hair, no hints of a budding moustache above his lip or of the more muscular form of some of his peers. He is quiet, watchful and rather opaque. In our opening group I sit next to him and feel his need for personal space. I move an inch or two to the left to create a gap. When he is introduced by a peer, they say he is kind, good to talk to and a loyal friend. I find myself wanting to know him better but immediately fear his circle of confidants might be very small. Does he find it hard to trust? I am intrigued.

Karl seems very self-conscious. His hands are wedged together on the table supporting his body, the tension visible in his white fingertips. When it is his turn to introduce somebody, he pauses. I fear he might be uncomfortable, but before my desire to rescue him takes over he speaks in measured but hushed tones. We all have to pay extreme attention to catch the words. I notice that it feels a relief to hear him speak and that the words he chooses to dispense feel like a gift. I am wondering how to make sense of him – is he using control as a way of coping with the pressure he feels? Perhaps he enjoys holding the space and making us wait. Or perhaps the opposite is true and he is struggling with the awful moment of giving voice?

Catching myself, I recognize how many assumptions I am making in the gap that he leaves when he acts in a way that doesn't immediately put myself or the group at ease. I am filling in that gap, trying to understand him. In doing so I will probably be getting a lot wrong. Any fixed assumptions I make now will waste time to unravel. I need just to be present, curious and observant but also true to myself, and above all try to understand the uniqueness of Karl.

Jazz is another member of the group and although 14 could pass for 20. Her hair and make-up proclaim her attractiveness, and her close-fitting clothes show off her mature model-like body. Jazz could be thought to announce a sexual certainty and appear very confident, but I notice that she seldom seems to be alone and always sits with her 'allies' next to her, one on each side, like two sphinxes. Around her peers, her desire to be quick in agreement with everyone is noticeable. Her eyes scan the group like a radar and then she seems to merge with what she finds, reflecting moods rather than creating them. Beneath the confident exterior there seems to be fragility and a desire to please.

Jazz seems particularly dependent on the boys for approval and I feel sad when I overhear the boys talking about her when messing around as a group, referring to her with derogatory terms: 'easy' and 'slag'. Karl surprises me as I overhear this exchange (a conversation not meant for my ears), when he speaks up to the boys in the group and says calmly, but with significant impact for its honesty, 'You shouldn't talk to Jazz like that. She is a good person.' Looks of surprise pass over the faces of the boys who made the remarks, and they change the subject, maybe out of embarrassment. Individually, one of them, Joe, remarks to me later in the day, 'That kid Karl, he is OK.' I wonder if the comment comes from a recognition of respect for Karl after he has spoken out, and maybe a wistfulness that Joe did not have the courage to challenge the group even though perhaps he knew he was just going along with the crowd. Perhaps he regrets insulting a girl who maybe is like himself, keen to fit in.

It's the beginning of another week and another group of adolescents have arrived; adolescents in all their colourful variety and stages of development. The word itself can have negative connotations and is sometimes used as a derogatory descriptor. In their frustration to comprehend their own children or the young people they work with, many people tar adolescents with broad brush strokes and apply words such as 'lazy', 'frustrating', 'moody', 'touchy', 'scary' or 'arrogant'. If our experiences are more rewarding, we might be likely to find them puzzling, confusing, interesting, funny, challenging and always changeable. The difficulty is that teenagers are often saturated with the challenges of their age. As mentioned in Chapter 2, neuroscience has informed us that adolescence is a period of opportunity and the quality of our relationships can help optimize development. But, as adolescents sometimes feel overwhelmed, although no longer so physically dependent on our care, they are emotionally in need of us as adults in more ways than they care to acknowledge.

Wherever we are with this age group, as a professional or a parent, we often feel at sea without a chart to help us navigate. It can feel like there is no solid ground and there are changes all around. We do our best to understand them but have no control over their emotions. We too can feel disappointment, humiliation, frustration, rage and fear. Our strategies that helped us feel 'in charge' for younger children are likely to no longer work and our best attempts at care and concern can be thrown back in our faces.

In many ways adolescents themselves are running on a parallel process: confused, changeable, searching. In addition, they are often thin-skinned, feeling vulnerable, uncertain and very sensitive to slights. They too are finding their way in uncharted seas. The task of their development can seem scary – the requirement to be reasonable and almost 'adult', while awash with the emotions they may well have felt as two-year-olds.

We were all there once, upon the brink of adulthood, trying to form our identities, while attempting separation from our parents, and turning towards facing the world as independent beings. Simultaneously, it is quite likely that we were feeling insecure about our looks, identities and performance at school, as well as working out our friendships and maybe even future roles. The world could feel judgemental and with very little compassion. Unless we were lucky, our friendships would be changeable and support systems invisible. When I was a teenager, I remember not speaking my inner thoughts to anyone, let alone my parents or siblings. Being an adolescent was a period of being secretive and wishing someone who understood would be there, while having an over riding feeling of trying very hard but never feeling good enough.

Providing support for young people during their teenage years is complex. Adding to this web, as we saw in Chapter 1 on cultural context, adults are having to accommodate and understand the pressures that exist for children in the 21st century, pressures that they themselves had no experience of at that age, alongside explanations and theories that might seem hard to agree with. Money, stress and self-image have all become related. Single parents make up one in four families in this country.[1] While doing their best, single parents, as well as those still together, are often under huge work pressures, and recreation as a family is often in short supply. Financial pressure rebounds on teenagers in more ways than one as they often want to own expensive brands of clothing to keep up with the tide of the times. Clothing is now about social status, showing which group you belong to, and comparisons are rife. Image is the consciousness that was always there for teenagers. Nowadays, however, with photos taken all the time, people's images are peddled on social media and this leaves them vulnerable to criticism all the time. Being judged can feel exposing and adolescents are very sensitive to the value that others place on them.

....

1   Gingerbread (2018) 'One in four: A profile of single parents in the UK.' Available at www.gingerbread.org.uk/wp-content/uploads/2018/02/One-in-four-a-profile-of-single-parents-in-the-UK.compressed.pdf (accessed 08/04/2020).

It is Day 2 on the farm and Jazz and Karl remind me of those challenges and contradictions that are key to the adolescent experience. Jazz looked so confidently dressed with her perfect make-up and coiffure, and yet at night when settling the group, I notice a big difference. She is very tactile with her friends, they groom each other's hair, pass compliments, joke around and play like kittens. Jazz shows me her perfectly made-up bed, her velvet heart-shaped cushion from home, and her teddy, well worn and cuddled. An hour later she is sucking her thumb, cuddling her bear and sleeping. The school have sent her because they are worried as her attendance is very poor. With her need for male approval, and lack of supervision at home, there is a worry she could be groomed and exploited, but they need to know more about her.

We discover Jazz is living with her father alone, and his way of showing his love to her is to give her money to buy clothes. While Jazz gets social approval for her clothes, her other needs for nurture may not be being met. Her girlfriends provide some sustenance, but her confidence is still low as she is confused about her self-image and who she wants to be.

Karl remains an enigma and yet on occasions when on the walks he lets down his guard and rolls down a hill, and by the time he reaches the bottom he is laughing, pink-faced and dishevelled. He is the first to cross the stream, balancing on a log, the first to help the teacher who is slipping in the mud. His natural chivalry, courage and desire for challenge is coming to the fore. There is a glimpse of the kindness and courage that his friend alluded to. But the full picture is more complex; we know from school that Karl is not flourishing. He lacks engagement, never puts his hand up or asks questions, and his teacher describes that he often seems to be in hiding in the classroom. He is a puzzle to them, and they hope to get some indicators to help him. Karl is not alone. Something essential has been missing for these children: play and nurture, confidence and relationships. Together with the teachers, our task is to build the teenagers' trust in themselves and their abilities as well as trust in adults so they can ask for help.

Puberty

Karl is one of the many young men who we discover is struggling with the frustration of comparing himself physically with some of his peers. The stage known as puberty references the biological changes and maturation of the body to adult form. Usually this is complete by 16 but young people like Karl are not unusual in the changes being delayed. Jazz is the opposite; her body has changed before her mind can catch up. She looks like a woman and feels like a small child.

Karl does not have the muscles of some of the lads in this group. Neither does he have the facial hair. He seems very young physically and has angelic looks. On the first day, I overhear some teasing about his 'baby face', his 'girl's' hair. It is hard to tell how these comments impact on him as he is so self-contained. It may also be that like some lads he will change beyond all recognition in the coming months as his physical development accelerates. His physical appearance manifests his feeling of individuality; his untypical long hair is contrast to the shaven sides and high quiffs of most of the boys in the groups. In some ways, although this marks him as an outsider of their friendship group, I feel they are quite keen to know his secret and how he does not need to conform, and there is growing interest in including him in their conversations and play.

Jazz is only six months older but is fully mature physically. Her breasts are fully formed, she has a defined waist and hips and her body communicates that she could bear children. She could be mistaken for an independent 18-year-old. I worry she could be taken advantage of or put herself in difficult situations as, although physically she has reached some developmental landmarks, she is nowhere near adult in her intellectual and emotional development. Conversely, her friend Ruby is pre-pubescent and, despite dressing as an adult, looks like a small girl. Ruby is bright, quick-witted and insightful, and can show maturity and perceptiveness when talking in a group. I hear her confide she would love to have periods and be as well developed as Jazz. When she voices her admiration of Jazz's good looks, it is as though she is bolstering Jazz's fragile ego with lots of compliments and reassurance, but there is a tiny tinge of envy.

In return, Ruby has found her value as protector. She uses her viper tongue to fend off insults from the boys. She may not yet have a woman's body but her mind is maturing. Her social intelligence is ahead albeit that her body is lagging.

Early adolescence brings shifts in body image and the confusion of new hormonal surges. Girls may start their periods and grow breasts and hips. Boys' voices deepen, their muscles seem to surge, they grow facial hair and often wear this like a badge of honour to be shared. Sometimes these changes may feel unwelcome. Nothing happens predictably or with any certainty; time accelerates for some children and lags behind for others. This fragmentation of development, of different rates of maturation, can affect the cohesiveness of the peer group, and this in itself can be unwanted change. Comparisons abound, and the individual's relationship to their body and mind can be fragmented. A child may resent being reminded of their future adult biology and feel frightened of its implications. The relative freedom of childhood is being replaced by yet another reminder that nothing will stay the same.

Approval

For most teenagers the people they most want to rate them, and whose approval they seek, are their friends. Peers' praise steps up to an even higher priority than previously. The child secure in feeling loved by a parent can afford to disappoint or frustrate this bond. The bond with a peer feels fragile, and approval is often used as a powerful tool by peers to dispense or dispose of when it suits their own needs. It can be easier to comply with peer pressure rather than face the potential rejection and humiliation. Peer pressure beats parental pressure and it helps when we accept this as adolescents become very vulnerable if they feel we minimize this knowledge.

It is hard to stay immune to the fashion or to sway from the values and interests of their own age group. These will often replace or render temporarily or permanently redundant the shared family interests or values, and the allegiance to clubs and mentors who led the way in the teenagers' younger years. The significant adults may appear to lose their charm. Those hours developing sporting prowess, interest in dance or drama, willingness to come on family holidays, joining in the clubs and extra-curricula activities of school, may all seem bafflingly denigrated by the teenager. For their peers, however, adolescents can light up, seem ready to play ball, put themselves out, make an effort and be appreciative. They seemingly make bad choices, join in 'unsuitable' activities, take crazy risks. As adults we may want to compete, but we have been demoted though probably not for ever or as fully as appearances may seem. In moments of need the child still needs the adult, for reassurance, practical reasons...and money! It can seem harsh that ten minutes after a row about a refusal to help put the bins out, a teenager can ask for a lift, or money for the latest trainers. But that is the normal switch of their brain, and in the moment it is important that we try not to over-react or become too judgemental in response.

Separation

Separation from adults, moving towards peer dependence

Separation from childhood and walking in the direction of adult independence is a tough road. On a good day a young person can feel omnipotent, blissfully unaware of danger and thus ready to take the road alone. On a bad day, they might want to crawl back into bed or shelter in the protection of an adult's care. When confident, they crave their peers; when frightened, they may crave their parents. One moment they may need you for comfort or help, but another time you might seem dispensable and unimportant. Their need for parental love may feel shameful and embarrassing to them. Friendship and romantic love become more important and adults become second best.

But separation is essential if a young person is going to transcend dependency. Independence means forming their own decisions, making their own mistakes, and finding their own way of making reparations when this happens. When they leave home, they will have to meet and greet the world without the protection of parents or key adult figures. They will choose their own friends and work, and perhaps create their own families. All of this may feel easier if there is a trial period, a time of coming and going between childhood and adulthood.

This can be a time to make mistakes but not be cast out. It is a time to change their minds, time to experiment, time to grow and learn. Ideally, as a foundation for this exploration, they need a secure base, with reliable adults to ground them and keep faith. Feeling a failure in the family as an adolescent makes it much harder to negotiate all the other challenges they face. For this reason, teenagers need us to believe in them, remain positive in face of their fears, be consistent and reliable, nurturing and understanding, and show optimism about their futures, especially when they feel in the dark.

Adolescents will possibly go back and forth at first, between extreme independence and retreating for hours into their rooms, with days sometimes spent in introspection. While we adults may feel that they do not care enough, perhaps what is actually happening is that they care too much: loyalty is a tension between the secure adults in their life and newly important friends and peers.

Importance of the family

Even within this context, with the increasing influence of the peer group, few children are not wounded by their own family being derided. Defensive love lies deep, even if not visible through the young person's actions. I have never met a child who did not still love their parent, even if they disliked them or, indeed, had reason to feel failed by them. Even the children of abusive or negligent parents still mostly feel a need to love that person. The 'loyalty' bond is tough and is a hard one to break. The insult that begins, 'Your mum...' is usually incendiary.

Karl's apparent insularity is disarmed one day.

Tyler, a self-appointed 'leader' in the group, is a large, well-developed boy of 14 and he seems bothered by the amount of praise Karl is receiving in the group for his honesty and his courage to try new things.

He takes a verbal swing at Karl: 'Your mum's a lazy b***h.' Karl rises from his chair and, in a moment, is incandescent with rage; he shoves Tyler sideways and Tyler falls on the floor.

'Don't you ever talk about my mum again or I will...'

The blow did not look very hard, but Tyler shouts, 'You broke my fucking shoulder, you faggot!'

The adults stand between the boys, managing to turn Karl towards the door and chaperone him out. Tyler struggles up with a helping hand. It is clear he has not broken his shoulder – he uses it inadvertently to climb back up to his chair. There is no look of pain as he bears weight on it, but he holds his arm to his chest as he lets go a volley of expletives about Karl being a 'nonce', a 'geek', and any other insult he can manufacture about him. Tyler seems to have forgotten he had struck the first blow, albeit verbally. He has used the most powerful insult in his armour and got a result. He has managed to get Karl to behave as he does; losing control makes them equal and Tyler needed to know he was vulnerable.

Once Karl has gone for a brisk walk, which has calmed

down his excess adrenaline, he begins to weep. The sadness beneath the torrent of rage is revealed. I understand anger is often protecting sadness and I recognize that Tyler's remarks were hard to bear. I ask Karl if he wants to share more about why and how those comments so powerfully upset him.

When out of sight of the group, Karl went on in a stuttering conversation to tell me about his mother. It seems she barely manages. She has been suffering from depression since his dad left two years ago, often not getting out of bed all day. He tells me she drinks a lot and that he is very anxious about her. Karl's description paints a picture of a life where he has had to become prematurely adult and the expected caring roles have been reversed. The effort of keeping his anxiety at bay about his mother leaves him full up and ready to burst. One jibe too many and he cannot contain himself. Tyler's remarks about his mother burst his bubble of containment and left him feeling undone.

He has revealed a very caring side, being tender with animals and younger children. This sensitivity disappears in front of his male peers.

Little did Karl know, but Tyler also struggles with feeling responsible for his mother. She is struggling to manage the family and he tells me that she is full of anger that Tyler's father has left her for another woman. Her pain seems to emerge as constant complaints and negativity taken out on Tyler. He tells me she asks him to look after his younger brothers but gets angry if they make a mess and blames Tyler for encouraging them and not setting a better example. He is expected to be older than his years, a father figure to much younger siblings, but has no male role model himself. He has maybe grown his 'macho' image to defend against his own feelings of helplessness.

On a walk the next day, Tyler and I have a moment walking together, just the two of us. He volunteers to me that he doesn't know why he attacks Karl verbally. He tells me that he actually thinks he's 'alright' and admits that a part of him respects Karl's difference. I remind him that he called him a 'faggot' and a 'nonce' and wonder what he feels about homosexuality. He turns, pauses, looks past me and says in a wistful way, 'A bit strange, I suppose, but maybe it's OK.' There is an expression of lostness, maybe a request for reassurance, and I wonder if this young man has ever been helped to consider his own sexuality.

Teenage tantrums

Like all teenagers, these young people are sometimes beset by emotions that are akin to their two-year-old or three-year-old self. Sometimes we witness 'tantrums' in a teenager that often resemble that blast of overwhelming passion that beset them as a two-year-old. Confusingly for their levels of intelligence, in the lull after the storm, they can change their mood, their direction of interest, and seem unaffected; and if we refer to their 'tantrum', they can even feel falsely accused. The adult may be left feeling damaged by the raging storm, while incredulous that teenagers can seem so in denial of the effects of their actions. They have moved on, are preoccupied by new challenges, and may resent an adult holding them to account for the past. This seems illogical, but the way their brains change tack can mean they live in the moment and feel there is no need to go back.

Tyler and Karl shared their vulnerabilities, but they may need to reconnect to their more familiar defended selves. I will need to move on with them; not remind them of their pain, but use the experience of their revelations as information to help me navigate the waters ahead. Defences grow as necessary protection; we can want a person to remain open and honest, but, in the world of peers and struggles with exposure, many teenagers produce a protective shell, often with a mask, and this provides a screen to hide behind for fear of being revealed and less defended.

Boundaries and language

I remember how as a parent it was easy to split (see below): too often I took the child's side, leaving my husband to be the disciplinarian. Later I was to learn that we represented the split inside the adolescent brains of our children: their logic and their impulses, and their struggle to unite these parts. In an ideal world we could be more helpful. As adults, if we can form a consensus, hold a line in unity, back each other up, then we might avoid feeding and exacerbating the confusion that already exists internally in the young person, and be more helpful to their overall development. We need to model being able to tolerate and process both the emotions and the logic.

When I think about that, I feel a sense of shame at my attempts to put logic in place of the wild emotions that sometimes took over my own children. For toddlers and through to adolescents, I frequently used a conversation of reasoning rather than a simple boundary with an empathic understanding. I often see very reasonable, caring and loving parents trying to use adult reasoning conversation with a three-year-old and wish that in their shoes I had realized that the child and myself would have benefited more from 'I can see you are upset but the answer is still no.' Hindsight would be a brilliant thing if we got to live our lives backwards! Now with grandchildren I have a lot of fun, but I am less afraid to lay down a boundary if empathy has failed.

Some of the new understandings from neuroscience would have brought helpful insight. Alongside this, I wish I had recognized that boundaries create safety, a container, and even if a child kicks, they need us to stand firm and be their rock in this tumultuous sea of change. Being willing to be disliked would be braver than needing to be loved. My need to be a liberal, consensual parent, alongside a less conscious need to act out my own inner rebel against authority, did me, my children and those I worked with no favours.

Splitting

Splitting is the psychological mechanism whereby we struggle to bring both positive and negative thinking together and resort to black-and-white thinking. Teenagers' brains resort to this simplification and act this out by creating a world where people are good or bad, loved or hated. They cannot cope with the grey areas of ambivalence as, on top of all they are dealing with, this can be difficult. At times, conversations may seem meaningless. The black-and-white version of a teenage world can frustrate our more developed adult minds. We speak of 'compromise' and 'measured risks' and encourage young people to see the other side. They may proclaim with passion that life is unfair, that a particular person is all bad, or that absolutely nothing can change. Part of the proneness to mood swings and strong emotions is because part of their brain is developing almost too fast (but will in time prune itself).

Splitting is seen in many forms of adolescent behaviour. Often, teenagers will try to split any adults who are caregivers, teachers or parents. We so often hear that one is favoured against another, the refrain: 'But, so and so says I could', 'How come everyone else is allowed to...', 'So and so's mother is much kinder/more generous/gives more freedom/understands...' As adults, it helps to stand firm, in agreement, to make sure we understand each other's lines and do not undermine each other.

It is bedtime and the girls seem to love to take time to nest. Maisie, who is in the group with Jazz and Ruby, is more introverted and loves reading. She has taken herself off, needing a break from the group and some time to be more insular. The older girls, Jazz and Ruby, take umbrage that they too are being asked to settle. They start to argue with the teacher, Miss Turner, and try to draw me in. It's not fair, they say, that their senior age isn't marked by privilege. They tell Miss Turner that Mr Jones, her co-teacher, agrees. The argument is strong, and they present it logically, ignoring the fact that Miss Turner has said several times that it is time to go up to bed. When she says she is not discussing it anymore, Ruby flips and starts shouting and hurling abuse at her teacher: 'You never respect us. It's not fair. This place is shit. You can't make me!' From being a happy relaxed child in front of the fire, playing with hair, we see a Harpie rise and volcanic rage.

Miss Turner is brilliant and sticks calmly to her guns. 'I am not arguing, Ruby, and that is the bottom line. It is bedtime and I hope you sleep well and tomorrow we can all embark on a fresh start,' and with this she walks away.

Ruby's battle is over if there is no one to fight, so reluctantly she gathers her stuff and with Jazz in tow retreats to bed.

By morning she is rested and acts as if nothing happened as she is living in the moment and ready to embark on the day.

Needs

In a group it is often difficult to process and respond appropriately to the differing needs of the teenager. Some enjoy more social time and have a greater appetite for talking, sharing and building friendships. Some are happy to settle to a game of chess or an interesting discussion, and may even help with practical chores. But some are still very motile and undisciplined, needing stimulation, perhaps because they struggle to reside in their own thoughts. Parenting or living/working with this age group requires us to be flexible and not judge them, and to dispense with too many preconceptions. Each child is unique, each with their own needs.

With the range of developmental tasks a teenager is processing, they are bound at times to feel overloaded. They need more sleep and their timing is often poor. They need good food but are often fussy feeders or indulge in sweets and fizzy drinks. They may be tired and sometimes irascible. Their day's work is largely psychological, internal, with no obvious benchmarks of success. No wonder they can feel overloaded when we make the smallest request.

Teenagers are striving to find their own identity, unique form and place, but all this is in a sliding landscape which is only just taking shape. While separating, they still yearn to belong. They crave familiarity but also change. They want freedom but still need boundaries.

On a bad day, adolescent anxiety is projected out, and

as adults we catch the flack. When we are feeling stronger, we manage not to react, not to take it personally. We can be patient and continue to believe in the young person, staying positive and strong, not being drawn into character assassination. Their moods are not their personalities and our reactions need to be proportional. Defining adolescents by their behaviours, labelling them or pronouncing judgement can only make things worse. If they feel we have no faith in them, their response is to give up on themselves. Positive belief systems and high expectations are more likely to guide them through. Adolescents are struggling and they need a hand to guide them through the difficult periods of their life and to help them come out feeling lovable with a sense of self-worth.

CHAPTER 4

Flight, Fight or Freeze

Humans still have animal instincts for survival, honed over millennia to help us adapt for maximum survival. Our instincts are to protect us from danger. While that danger may not be in the form of being attacked by animal predators, we protect ourselves from being hurt, be it physically or emotionally, with our elaborate defence mechanisms. Defences fall broadly into ways in which we simulate some sort of fight reaction, take flight, or freeze. Teenagers demonstrate these defences in a multiplicity of ways; often raw and vulnerable as they are, their defence system can be hypervigilant and over-reactive. Living and working and sharing time with them exposes us as adults to a myriad of their behaviours that can confound, challenge and dismay us. Interpreting these behaviours as communication and learning the language of defence systems can help bring us understanding, tolerance and empathy for the young person, and for ourselves.

Frequently we are confounded by what can appear over-reaction or stubbornness in a child. We can feel they are deliberately blocking us, or even over-dramatizing to get attention. So many of the signals are misleading and we get ourselves into a tangle and place of opposition. Frustration and feelings of inadequacy arise on both sides, in the adult and in the child. Situations can escalate, and good intentions disappear. We become lost in a struggle or battle and the antecedents are lost or forgotten.

Babies are not born prickly or brittle. In their first cries to express their needs, they are not being aggressive. A crying baby who is hungry is not being 'demanding'; they are letting us know their need. When a baby is in pain, their cry is to communicate, not to harass us. When they are frightened and need holding, they are not 'clingy and demanding'. They might just need reassurance. From the moment a baby enters the world, we can start to apply labels that might define them.

The relationship between parents/adults and children will always feel precarious, with us doing our best to provide nurture, but with patterns inevitably being set in motion according to our own experiences. This is not to say there is no such thing as 'character' or nature, but in the mix we may underestimate the adaptations that happen as part of humans' instincts to survive the individual family circumstances and environment into which we are born. In the children we have met so far in this book, we see how their adaptations can become impediments restricting them from thriving. Their coping mechanisms and personal defence systems, which were once developed to protect them from too much emotional pain and discomfort, can become a burden, an impediment to their happiness.

As adults, we too are not immune to the need to have systems for protection, and many of these remain subconscious defence mechanisms. It is often only when they cease to work, when we hit a crisis or receive challenging honest feedback and reflect, that we see our similarities to children. When I work with children, I recognize my own adaptation to life, my own forms of flight, fight and freeze. At times I fear that I am inauthentic, that I have become a chameleon and play the roles ascribed to me in my family when I was young. It is natural that parts of us hide for fear of being shamed. We might 'people please' for fear of rejection. We can become a clown or a distractor as a means of deflecting attention from our vulnerable selves. We can become controlling when we are anxious. When relating to children and adults, we often see characteristics that might have been originally for adaptation to circumstances and have then become embedded as their 'character'.

There are many ways of describing defence mechanisms, but working with children I find it most helpful to see them in terms of flight, fight or freeze. Children are instinctive, and the notion of, as humans, our need for 'animal' survival can help us understand and be less judgemental. We see how some children are triggered to take **flight** in forms of emotional withdrawal, which may look like avoidance or denial. It may also be physical: running or moving away; not going to school; staying for hours in their bedrooms. Some may choose **fight** and become aggressive to ward off danger. They may act 'big', being loud, angry and defiant. Alternatively, in the face of threat, fear and psychic pain, some may even **freeze**, shut down, become numb and dumb, or go under the radar, hoping for invisibility.

Flight

Horses are flight creatures. Along with most herbivores they are prey to carnivores and on the lookout for danger. To escape is to bolt, to run with the herd heading for safety. Children take flight, follow the mood of the crowd, hide in the 'herd' or emotionally withdraw. A challenge that feels too great, a moment of shame, an embarrassment or exposure, all of these may trigger a need to protect themselves. Practised from childhood, defences begin to flourish. Some are subtle, some crude, but the instincts that alert them are all about survival and gain without pain.

Deflection as a form of flight

I hear Tyler say, 'I'm bored', but I am wondering if he means 'I fear failure'. The task ahead feels intimidating. Spending time with Tyler has taught me that he prefers not to show his vulnerability. And why should he, as he fears being ridiculed by his peers and does not yet trust adults? We are about to go on a hike and he has heard there is a mountain to climb. Tyler likes to look strong and brave, but I have noticed he has lots of ways of opting out of challenges. I am wondering if his physical stamina is not as great as he likes to make out or if he is fearful of the unknown (being in the countryside itself is so unfamiliar to him). He may fear heights and the group have been egging each other on with bravado and talk of cliff edges and high peaks (neither of which exist on this hike, but their imaginations like to exaggerate). Joe grumbles, 'What's the point in this?' Is this a disguise for 'I won't be able to manage this task'? I have watched Tyler change the subject, cause a distraction, set up a smoke screen, all as a deflection; maybe this is his best way of fleeing from the moment or from the focus of discomfort.

I feel sad for Tyler because by maintaining his mask of invulnerability he is struggling alone. Worse still, he gets to be unpopular with staff as he is experienced as disruptive and obstructive. I hear him described by some of the girls in the group as 'selfish'. Arguments create trails of deception, leading away from the core of his difficulties; he hides his lack of confidence.

Many of the children I have met in the classroom, in a therapy situation and in social interactions find ways of deflecting. Not many of us are confident enough to say with honesty, 'I feel rubbish at this task and fearful that the rest of you will show me up.' Much easier to say that I am not interested, it's not my thing or this is badly taught. I remember well my own lack of interest and disengagement with subjects I found hard as a child. As a teenager it was much easier to mess around in class, avoid attending or make fun of the teacher; anything but say how small and stupid I felt in comparison to my peers who found those subjects easy. It felt so hard to ask for help.

Without feeling safe, trusting of an empathic relationship, it is easier to be stubborn, resistant, avoidant. These are all means of withdrawing and taking flight. Sadly, for Tyler there are times at school when his behaviour has been taken at face value. His behaviours that were adaptive have become a barrier, a maladaptation taken to the new and different circumstances. With a week away from the normal triggers of home and school we are beginning to see there are different versions of Tyler. He is more able to allow adults to come alongside and be more supportive. He lets down his mask of invulnerability. He is more open to honest engagement and allows some support. He acknowledges that his life is hard, and he can feel fearful and uncertain; even that maybe it is easier to say he does not want to do something than to say he might need some support and feels unconfident that he will succeed.

Withdrawal

Withdrawal may be second nature to a child who does not have a secure and loving base to ground them, or one whose life feels overwhelming with challenges which are too hard to meet. Karl is one such child; when overwhelmed by his responsibilities at home, he preferred to withdraw and not trust engagement. On first meeting him, he seemed closed and withholding, but gradually we learnt he had a lot to offer and needed time and space to begin to relate. He is building a friendship with Janine, aged 13. They seem to instinctively recognize in each other some of the same ways of dealing with their difficult lives. Janine has grown up in a family where her parent has modelled withdrawal as a way of being. Her mother struggles with mental health; her depression sometimes overwhelms her and she retreats to bed. Janine is fearful for her, and has heard at school about another mother's suicide. On meeting Janine, she seems very shy and under-confident, and when invited to take part in any activities she hangs back and is hard to engage. I am puzzled and ask her teacher, Heather, how she is at school. Heather is thoughtful, and then reflects that Janine has often come to her complaining of stomach aches or headaches; she also seems to miss a lot of classes, presenting herself to the school nurse. At first it was because she was struggling with periods, but maybe this is not the case as she turns up too often. Heather and I wonder if this could be a cry for help, a way that Janine expresses her pain. We remind ourselves that somatizing emotion is common; the pain is real, and may be a displacement of the emotional hurt. It could be Janine has abdominal migraines in the way some people have headaches, triggered when she feels confused or vulnerable. How else can she show her pain?

Heather teaches Janine weekly. Her relationship might be an important support in the future. She makes the effort to sit with her at mealtimes, shares stories of the day's activities and includes Jazz, who she knows has a kind heart but is also struggling with a difficult home. On a walk they drift into their own group, and swap stories of some of the things they find hard. Heather gives them space, walking a few steps ahead. It seems the girls acknowledge their anxieties. Later in the day Janine acknowledges that it's the first time she has ever been able to talk about home to anyone else. Heather is able to say that if Janine would appreciate it, she could have a confidential space at school to see a counsellor to share some of her worries. Janine pauses, looks away and then gives a small smile. 'Yes, please,' she says.

Janine, like many children, has not had the space at home to share her thoughts and feelings. We meet other children whose parents withdraw into a drug- or alcohol-induced state whenever they feel life is too much. They have modelled withdrawal from reality as a normative response to stress. If the support for a family is in short supply, a child has little chance to process their own needs and feelings.

Withdrawal may be a defence mechanism triggered by trauma. An abusive relationship, violent parents, bullying siblings, overly dependent or intrusive or controlling parents, can all result in a child withdrawing. Withdrawal may become a reflex reaction and then a pattern and sadly end up as a behaviour that gets embedded.

Another week at the farm and I meet Mario, who in some respects reminds me of Karl. He speaks with a quiet voice, muffled so I have to strain to hear. It is as if he feels his words are insignificant, not worthy of full volume. He gazes out from under a long fringe, watchful, yet very still. In the group he can merge into the background, easy to miss, and his teachers say he often goes under the radar. His grades are 'good enough', but there are long periods of absenteeism. Recently the school have been concerned as his behaviour is occasionally erratic and he seems to linger in the school, not wanting to go home. His parents have failed to come to any parents' evenings and the school has wondered if this is due to a language problem as they are recent residents in England.

It is towards the end of a week and Mario has begun to emerge daily with newfound confidence both to do new things and express himself. We take my dog for a walk. He starts by commenting on the peace of the countryside. I ask how it compares to his life in North London. It seems he does not know his area well as he only goes out to shop for his mum and go to school. We continue our walk and observe a group of sheep quietly grazing, with some ewes lying down and their lambs nestled beside them. As we approach, a ewe rises to her feet, grows tall and stamps her feet at my approaching dog. I comment that she is very protective of her young and we must give her space and respect her good instincts. Mario comments under his breath, 'I wish my dad would give my mum space.'

He hangs his head. We pause, leaning on a gate. 'I am wondering if that troubles you,' I say. Mario looks up and then with passion explodes and hits the gate with a stick. The sheep leap to their feet and move to the other side of the field. 'Yes,' he says, looking at me for the first time. 'My dad comes home drunk, with his friends. I know it will always end up in arguing and fighting…' His voice trails off and suddenly he looks very small and withdrawn. 'I imagine it is very hard for you,' I say. 'Perhaps it makes you both angry and then a bit helpless as they are much bigger than you.' 'Yes,' he says, 'I wish I could protect my mum, but she says it's better I stay in my room and keep out of it.'

'Keeping out of it' has become a way of life for Mario, but a very sad and lonely one. We return across the fields, and before we get back he turns and says, 'Thank you.' I tell him I am relieved to see him angry as things that upset us make us angry or sad, and sometimes we get stuck in the sadness. He returns a smile and we walk on and I notice there is more spring in his step. Perhaps he has lightened his emotional load.

Avoidance

Avoidance is a good protection, a way of taking flight out of the range of danger or discomfort. It might be better not to try than to fail. Or is it better to show lack of interest than to give something a go, prove yourself inadequate? Most of us know that feeling of giving up, making excuses, feigning lack of interest if we are in a situation that we feel is too challenging. Jazz does avoidance by getting lost in the crowd. She joins the melee and becomes like a bee in a swarm, avoiding predators by being one of a crowd, hoping she cannot be picked off for attack.

She gets silly and flighty, merges with the behaviour of others, joins in but does not stand up to be counted. She is in hiding, deep down afraid of being 'found out'. She does not know what she believes in, and is aware she agrees with anyone for fear of being unpopular. She is embarrassed and fearful, knowing she lacks her own identity.

Projection

Projection is another form of flight away from our own inner anxieties or discomforts. It is classic to be aware of 'faults' in others that mirror something that we feel uncomfortable about in ourselves. Do we see others as greedy when we fear our own appetite? Are we annoyed by loud/jokey people but are rather shy ourselves and a bit envious of their confidence? Is that other parent at school seen by you as over-zealous at helping their children with homework because you find it hard to get time to help your children? Do you criticize people who smoke and drink too much but struggle to control your own urges?

Girls are particularly known for their 'bitchiness', which often takes a form of projection. Ruby could be the ringleader in this respect: a moral adjudicator, judgemental on the surface, envious beneath: 'She is a flirt', 'So and so loves to be the centre of attention', 'She just wants to be part of the popular group'. All these qualities seemed to belong to her but in her discomfort, she would disown these parts of herself and see them in others. She hated it when teachers took control at the times she was playing the lead. Leading was a quality Ruby had to have to survive her chaotic life but sometimes it led her to clash with teachers. I nearly collided with her myself, as my patience wore thin; at times I disliked her omnipotence. It was only after I had a chance to connect with Ruby in some horse work that I realized how hard she had to work inwardly to sustain herself in the absence of supportive parents. Maybe a part of me was envious of her popularity and centrality in the group, a place I never held at her age. Owning or taking back my own projection freed me to like Ruby more and work more sympathetically.

Denial

Denial is one of the strangest defences. This form of taking flight from reality seems to make the world more manageable. Sandra, one of the teachers, is talking about Tyler, thinking about how she can better understand him. 'How is it,' she says, 'I can watch him upend a chair, disrupt a lesson, chuck a rubber and yet when I call him out, he denies he has done anything and says I am always picking on him? This behaviour is maddening! I tell him, "But I saw you with my own eyes!" Once in victim mode he makes out it is my fault, that I am choosing to get at him.'

We think about Tyler together and wonder if both his denial and displacement serve to protect his fragile self that cannot bear to be in the wrong. In a given moment, any child really can believe his or her own lie: 'I didn't do it.' The more the lie gets forced into the open by a teacher, the harder an alternative truth in the child's mind get fixed. The new script, feeling attacked, blamed and undermined by the teacher, has taken over.

Sandra admits she finds it crazy-making that children can lie so blatantly. 'How is it possible,' she asks, 'when lying is something we are taught from a young age is wrong?' Lying is also denying reality. As adults we like to believe we have a handle on what really happens. Living in the grey areas of the unknown can be uncomfortable. Thus, the child who lies can drive us mad.

Later in the day I am reminded of my own reactions to children, as a teacher, when they bewildered me with their capacity to deny reality; and yet now, as a grandparent, I am reminded of how much of a fantasy world children live in, how often it is a safe place to retreat to, and how stories we tell ourselves can feel true as long as we want or need to believe in them enough.

Fight

A dog that barks and snarls may have its aggression more often triggered to protect its young or its owner, rather than because of a pure desire to attack. It is often fear that triggers the growl. Some children are like animals (for example, cats or fish) that literally puff themselves up to seem bigger and less vulnerable. Verbal aggression can be showing their hackles like a dog, a warning sign: 'Keep away, I am not safe.' None of this is triggered if we are not feeling threatened. In an altercation, in the classroom, or in the street, or at home, we forget how easily we may stimulate the fight mechanism in another. We may up the ante by becoming more hostile ourselves. We may resort to louder voices, verbal threats of punishment, cornering a person verbally or intimidating them. All this increases the chances of them feeling the need to defend themselves, and their most likely form of defence is their own fight response.

The chances are that a child in fight mode will be fuelled

by an adrenaline rush and flooded with cortisol, all of which in turn clouds any clear thinking. Often a lifetime of triggers or lack of safety has put the child into this aggressive mode.

Children in their triggered states need to be soothed and calmed to a point that they can re-engage. They may need space, time, reassurance... anything but fuel for the fire. They may need to digest the adrenaline with vigorous activity before being able to re-engage or even talk sense.

Sarah came to the farm as part of a group of disaffected girls. They were causing problems in school. Some were openly defiant and contradictory, some were stubborn and unwilling to join in, some seemed to be following in the wake of these powerful forces and getting caught up in the current. As a group, they were controlling and hard to like, challenging in their insulation and apparent lack of interest in others. I particularly struggled with the ringleader, Sarah. She had been referred because of getting into fights with other girls and swearing at teachers.

I had been on the receiving end of the apparent power of girls like Sarah when a child myself. Moving primary school every few years, spending six months in a school in England before then returning to East Africa, I lived life as the 'outsider'. I had to develop ways to deal with the vulnerability I felt. Girls like Sarah set off my alarm bells and made me feel ready to take flight or fight. Sarah reminded me of the girls who controlled the group at my school and who kept me as the outsider, feeling somehow inadequate, awkward, lonely and ashamed of my need to be liked. I wanted Sarah to be different. I wanted to be the one who could soften her and find her vulnerability, or who could stand up to her and not be intimidated. I didn't trust her power and I disliked seeing her manipulate the other girls. Either way, I was too invested, personally triggered and too ready to do battle. I needed to stand back and try to understand Sarah as an individual, not as a challenge, not someone to control as she controlled others. Moreover, I had to remember I was part of a team; it was not all down to me.

I was wary. I needed to remind myself of past lessons when I had fallen into my own trap with girls presenting control and aggression. I had the benefit of experience. I needed to pause, reflect, be curious. Why did Sarah need to protect her role as ringleader and have such a hard exterior? She seemed so 'fake' when she arrived, literally wearing a mask of make-up. She was carefully constructed and matched her hair style to all the girls in the group. Despite her look of disdain and superiority, her quick temper, her need to argue with adults and be a vocal protector of friends, I also recognized those tell-tale signs of possible anxiety: often downcast eyes, nibbled fingernails, bottom lip chewed. Sarah was a lioness who was protecting her cubs (the group). She was on guard, ready to fight as a defence; but who was protecting her?

Soothed by having time to inwardly reflect and remember that this young woman was not born like this, that somehow this persona was probably an adaptation to her particular life circumstances, I searched for a positive. In our first conversation, I remarked that she was generous in the time and energy she gave to looking out for her friends. I complimented her for the qualities that were evident: her willingness to come to a smelly farm, to leave the security of home territory, to give up her comforts – phones and sweets. I commented that she seemed a brave young woman, a leader, and I recognized that sometimes that is tiring and a pressure. Sarah gave me her first tentative eye contact and almost a look of surprise. This was not how she expected to be greeted. Clearly, she was more used to animosity, but she was willing to risk another way.

Sarah, hesitant but tempted, entered the spirit of the farm: the positivity, friendship, patience of the adults and above all nurture. Animals took her outside her comfort zone. She said she felt 'at home'. She unravelled her defences and became more spontaneous. She splashed in puddles and got covered in mud. She helped her teacher across the stream and found her a stick to help support her sore knee. She tended a sick lamb. Sarah surprised herself. She was in new territory and those very carefully crafted defences of a lioness began to become less activated. The triggers of fear and protection were not required on the farm. She began to relax. The make-up and mask were no longer needed to give an impression of fierceness and invulnerability. A childish spontaneity and sense of fun and playfulness emerged.

Day 3 on the farm is the time when children have settled in. They have absorbed the shock of the new. They have found their feet. Subconsciously they may need to see if we can really like them if they test us out. This world needs to prove its robustness. The people have to prove they are trustworthy. Sarah is getting tired and she is losing the power over her friends as they have taken off on their own journeys of transformation. The quieter ones are speaking up more, showing their independent thinking. Her closest allies are drifting into new alliances. All this is threatening to Sarah. She refuses to go on the walk. She becomes belligerent. She tries to persuade the others to follow suit, but one by one they choose to go. Sarah is alone and tearful.

Her former castle is in disrepair. I ask if she would like to help me put the chickens to bed. No, she does not want to do anything. 'That's OK,' I say. 'Maybe you are feeling tired and a bit dispirited, fed up. Things are changing and that is tough.' I chat away to her about remembering some of the good things she has done this week, also saying how difficult it is to give up ways of being as they have often served us well. Maybe it is hard being left behind. If she liked, I could give her a lift in the Land Rover, and we could catch up with the group.

Sarah is up and out of her chair, off to get her boots. She has been allowed to change her mind. The choice feels hers. She puts her energy into moving forward rather than resistance. I have had to be mindful of not making it feel like a trap; instead it is an open door I am offering.

Later that evening in our 'check-in', Sarah says she is glad she came on the walk. Her friends say how proud of her they are that she chose to come. They like this new, softer Sarah. They will look out for her. Sarah is letting go of her defences, peeling off her mask, beginning to feel safe enough to build real friendship, dispensing with the version built on fear and coercion.

In her one-to-one conversation, as we walk the dog, Sarah describes her family. Dad has left. He no longer wants to see her and her two younger brothers. He has a new baby. Mum is depressed. She feels rejected. Sarah is overwhelmed with responsibility and feels rejected herself. She is aware that she is 'every teacher's worst nightmare', as she feels no adults care or like her – so she has nothing to lose. Tentatively Sarah admits she would like to trust teachers and adults, but realistically she says, 'It's going to be difficult.' This feels like a new beginning, tentative and hopeful.

Before Sarah leaves the farm on Friday, we talk to the staff about offering her ways of expressing her leadership qualities positively rather than negatively in the school, in ways she can get enrichment from praise and recognition, rather than disapproval for being bossy. Her teachers that have accompanied the visit speak of now liking her, wanting to be her advocate, of better understanding, of a desire to change others' opinions of Sarah; they are now on her side. She may no longer need to have such a fight defence. She may be able to rediscover being a child.

Freeze

Freeze is the final and often underestimated defence we use to protect ourselves. It works. When life is tough, we sometimes become muffled in a shroud of numbness. Better not to feel anything than be overwhelmed. A small child may look like a rabbit in the headlights as their parents fight or argue. A boy who is being bullied curls up and shuts down and lets the physical or verbal punches ricochet off his body or his mind. The girl who has just lost her mother to cancer sits at the back of the class, seems glazed over, unfeeling, but trapped in her aloneness and barren wasteland. These children are not like the baby bird that feigns death in shock; rather they freeze in more subtle ways, looking normal from the outside, possibly a bit robot-like, but inwardly defensive, becoming numb.

The cause can be trauma, either persistent chronic damage or a single traumatic event. Dissociation is a relief, like losing the sensation from the cold in your feet. It is a survival strategy and, though good to protect, there can be lasting damage.

As humans rather than animals, our freeze can be triggered by emotional anxiety. Sometimes there is only so much we can bear. Too much and the brain dissociates, and the chill takes away the fear. Sometimes it is better to be numb and appear dumb. In some ways Karl was a frozen child, inaccessible and remote, unemotional and still, but within the warmth of the community he began to thaw and emerge.

Frozen children can easily go under the radar as they are less likely to attract attention than the potentially explosive child. They share a lot of characteristics with children in flight, and indeed, a freeze response to stress is part of the continuum of a desire to protect. Alternatively, they can be experienced as frustrating, as if holding power in their cold war, inaccessible and mysterious, seemingly strong.

I am reminded of a girl who was diagnosed as selectively mute. She was from a big family, stormy and chaotic, where apparently, according to her teacher, it looked as if the loudest got most attention. Molly had gradually shut down in this family. She had become quiet and withdrawn, but her silent presence had a big effect. Her teacher described how her parents and siblings were expressing frustration and bewilderment, upset by her refusal to converse. Anyone she met might be drawn into the compulsion to try and get her to talk. Alternatively, in her family, she could get given up on, left in peace.

I was curious about whether Molly's muteness was a result of trauma and a freeze response, or was it her creating the desired effect of power in a family where she might feel powerless? Maybe, as often happens, it was a reaction to a combination of causes, not a single trigger. I wondered if her defiance of silence was insulating her. Or could it be a smoke screen, an obfuscation of her real internal feelings of anger and hurt? It seemed Molly for the most part remained silent, but with one of her siblings she could chatter away. The picture was, and seldom is, simple.

The challenge was to accept Molly as she was and avoid the temptation to think that making her speak was a sign of success. We had to find ways of showing enthusiasm for just being in her company, positivity for her achievements, warmth, friendship and, above all, acceptance that she was doing what felt right for her.

On a walk I thanked Molly for her lovely company and told her I had enjoyed sharing the peace of the countryside with her, which was genuinely true. Once I got over my own need to communicate verbally, and the discomfort of silence, I could appreciate Molly's choice to be silent and the world on our walk was anything but silent; it was full of birdsong, the background chatter of the group and distant noises of the world humming along.

Later, working alongside Molly, feeding the pigs, it was possible to think out loud: 'I notice I am curious to understand how you feel, Molly: if you mind these snorting animals with their grunting and their smells.' A shake of her head and I think she is saying it is alright; she smiles and laughs as one piglet runs through her legs, keen to be fed first, declaring its unashamed appetite.

In the group, adults and children gave 'shout-outs' to Molly, along with the rest of the group, which helped her feel valued just as she was: 'The lambs have loved your calm and the way you tune into their needs.' 'The food you cooked was delicious, thank you.'

Her teacher warmly said she loved her smile, it lit up her

morning; her friend Jemima remarked on her strength; Jo chuckled and blurted, 'Bet you are real strong,' and Molly's smile broadened.

In the group, during check-ins, Molly began to take her turn. At first a hand with fingers for numbers, gradually a few words. Small steps, yet significant – Molly was beginning to take an equal part. The boundaries gave her safety, the format provided a pattern, taking turns moved the spotlight. This 'family' helped make her feel safe, its unwritten rules gave her space. Molly began to emerge, safe enough to thaw out, unfreeze.

Molly began talking again when she felt safe, albeit quietly. She now had the support of her peers, and the three teachers, who were now her advocates. She gradually blossomed over the week. She found a shift in her friendships and in the ways teachers treated her and their expectations of her. Molly had begun to thrive as a participant of a community rather than an observer.

After her visit, during a follow-up at school, we heard she shifted almost imperceptibly and by the end of term her parents were able to comment on having the pleasure of Molly as a central part of the family. She was taking her place actively, rather than passively; she expressed her needs and desires; she competed with her siblings in a healthy way; and her anger, when triggered, was expressed, not repressed. Beneath that quiet, there was a quick-witted, clever girl who surprised all with her perceptiveness and abilities. I was reminded never to underestimate the person beneath the behaviour, to read the behaviour itself as a communication.

Defences are like overcoats: taken off when the environment warms up and we no longer need them. When a child feels like they are taking flight, or need to show their hackles or dumb down their reactions, I try to ask myself: 'Why this, why now?' My curiosity is not always rewarded with answers, but it holds open the door to being less judgemental and believing that there is probably a good reason why someone behaves in the way they do.

CHAPTER 5

Communication

'I'm drowning not waving!'

Kia is angry, shaking with rage, heart racing, hands and head in a sweat, pacing and cursing. He is like a raging bull. People stand back, scared and alert. Kia is muttering and cursing and then spinning round. Flailing and shouting, he is ready to hit out.

Kieran looks worried and is wanting to run. He has set this in motion and has nowhere to hide. He knows it's his fault but it's too late to turn it around.

Two boys messing about and a comment that was too harsh has triggered Kia into rage. 'Your mum...' said with any other insult is poisonous and charged. Both boys are fiercely defensive of their mothers; we know from their school there are no dads on the scene. It feels like their job to be the 'man around'; and inadequate though they may be, they will defend their mothers' honour.

Kia is raging on the outside; is he crying within? He has expressed to his tutor that he is exhausted by protecting a mother who is struggling to survive. Maybe he is at his limit himself, and Kieran, his best friend, over a scrap about football, has stuck the dagger in. I imagine Kieran was embarrassed, having kicked an own goal, and possibly in shame has retaliated and deflected his feelings, translating them into blame. He has blamed Kia for the incident and called out an insult as well; the distraction is perfect.

So much happens so fast we can be left bewildered by the whirlwind of emotion. The boys need space to calm down. They need to de-escalate and release. We may not know the full reasons for this explosion. For now, it's enough to recognize they are both hurting inside and displaying this as anger. Understanding the emotion beneath the behaviours may take time. Blame and reasoning will not help, but space from each other will, and an adult recognizing that something important is behind the explosion would be a good start. We need to begin with their reality and work from there.

So often we find things are not all they seem. There is a gap between what is said and what is meant, what is done and what is felt. Behaviour is a signal, sometimes a red light or a code. If possible, we can frame all behaviour as communication, decode the messages and then search for an appropriate response. The child who is shouting and violent may be internally panicking and crying out for help. The girl who self-harms may be furious at the world but fearful to show it. The boy who looks arrogant and aloof may be shy and feel awkward. The child who hides in their room and won't engage in family life may be full of worries they cannot explain. The only way to discover the authentic person behind the mask is to be patient, curious, observant, creative and kind. But sometimes we too are exhausted, fed up, full up with our own stresses and anxieties. Willingness to try, even if we fail, can bring dividends, signal concern and begin to change things for the better.

Walking into a large London comprehensive at 8.30 one morning, I saw the smiling head teacher greeting children, saying: 'Hello', 'How was the weekend?', 'Like your new hair style', 'Great new bag', 'Good to see your smile on a Monday morning'... My day felt peppered with brightness, a ray of sunshine crossing the school lobby. This contrasted with the previous day when I walk through the revolving door from outside the huge block that looks like a factory but is in fact a secondary school; there is a sharp contrast between birdsong and the shouting of the teacher. I saw a pupil with his back against the wall, his friends gathered with smirking faces, the young man's face stiff with resentment and rage as he was lambasted for having no school tie, for repeatedly being late, for not looking at the teacher as he spoke to him! Inwardly I felt my own anger rising and a desire to verbally decimate and humiliate the teacher in the manner he was doing to the child in front of him. Help! I had been swiftly netted in the cycle of negativity. I had jumped to the side of the child who I know nothing about and polarized the teacher.

Being human, we tend to take sides with the person with whom we most empathize. The pupils witnessing this scene may react with their own programming: 'It's not fair', 'Stupid rules', 'Stupid teachers, always looking to blame/bully and tell someone off.' Others may feel: 'He is getting what he deserves... Serves him right.' Already, at the beginning of the day, expectations have been put in motion and many of these are negative.

Teachers and pupils are alike, as are parents and children; all of us need to have our reality recognized, to be met with empathy, to feel liked and appreciated. How we meet and greet each other sets in motion patterns, our deeper expectations of positive or negative outcomes. Feeling liked or appreciated often stirs a reciprocal feeling. Expectations beget more expectations. A tone is easily set at the beginning of every interaction. For example, we can arrive home tired from work:

...grumbling about the weather, the state of the hallway as we wade through cast-off shoes, calling out to the children accusingly, 'You could at least have put your coats and shoes away,' and the evening is off to a poor start for all.

Or we can say:

'Whew, how good to be home – it's awful weather out there. Hope you dodged the storm. How are the spirits of the troops? I am whacked, but tell me about your day. I hope you had a good one.'

Imagine, it's a school day, you are a new teacher, and you wake, the alarm banging in your ear drums, raise your head off the pillow and recognize the symptoms of a hangover. Damn, you should not have drowned your sorrows yesterday, on a school night, but then it was such a disappointment. You had failed your driving test for the third time. All that expense. Still going to have to take the bus to work. And now, it's so early yet time to get moving or you will be late.

Just by the skin of your teeth you arrive at school on time, but the headteacher looks frazzled, is pacing up and down, and greets you by saying she needed you here half an hour ago.

Samantha's mum has been on the phone. She is frantic. Samantha did not come home till very late last night. Her mum asks for the school to let her know who she is hanging around with. The headteacher turns on her heel and marches off, head down.

You feel a double dose of stress. You wanted some sympathy from the head about your disappointment. Instead you get dumped with another layer of responsibility. Your own stress from the rush to get here, the head's for the girl. On top of this, you have your own mixture of reactions. You felt Samantha was doing so well. You had a bond with her and she was attending school well but had been getting involved with some of the 'popular' girls and started applying layers of make-up, looking much older than her years. Now you are worried. Who has she been with? What negative influences is she vulnerable to? You feel both anxious and let down. The cocktail of feelings makes your sickness from the hangover feel worse. You enter your form room looking preoccupied, miserable and irritated. Your class looks up – each child has their own different internal reaction.

Sam thinks to himself, 'Here she comes, bad day look, I am going to get the hell out of here if I can.'

Ruby: 'Oh, no, she looks cross. I can't trust her to tell her about Jo bullying me on the way to school.'

Ali: 'Yet another miserable teacher. They are so boring.'

Jack: 'What have I done NOW! Brace yourself, she is going to blame me, she always does.'

So many crossed wires and competing needs for understanding. This is daily life. Events and feelings bump into each other and stress becomes a virus infecting others. We have failed to start in the way that we need to, to process our reactions and not let them spill over and pollute the waters of others. No one here has acknowledged anyone's feelings.

There are many defence mechanisms that we commonly use to make life feel more manageable. Projection is so common, displacing our discomfort or dislikes, seeing them in others. Children do this instinctively, blaming others and thereby displacing their own needs or discomforts so as not to overload themselves with difficult feelings. They may even want to rescue or champion other people, but beneath this they crave that response for themselves.

How often do we hear complaints or blaming of another and recognize that the complainer is out of touch with themselves? Everyday life brings its trials and tribulations, leaving us, as children or adults, unsettled, frustrated, unhappy or angry, and we can so often blame others for our feelings and contaminate them with our own corrosive feelings.

How often do we meet with a friend, try to communicate with a child, or enter a work situation, enveloped in deep frustration and possible annoyance? Our interactions can be polluted by our feelings; the inside of us is seen as belonging to the other. 'Why are they so touchy?' you might think. 'Why are they so angry, so irritable?' We project our lens onto the other, and blame them for how we are feeling, or at least displace our feelings and see the other as the carrier.

Have you had a bad day at work and then blamed the children for making you feel worse as they have left their rooms in a mess?

Are you struggling with your weight and then getting furious that your daughter is failing to eat sensibly?

Did your partner come home tired and you blamed them for being lazy when you are playing the martyr and insisting on clearing up the house when you are exhausted?

Are you anxious about your child's GCSE results and pushing them to work harder because you did not do as well as you hoped at their age?

Back to the school – let us imagine a re-run.

The headteacher sees you coming through the door. She has a smile on her face and asks how you are and whether you passed the driving test as she knows how important this was for you. You acknowledge feeling disappointed, having a sore head and regretting that, and ask for any important updates with school. The head expresses her concerns about Samantha, explains that there will be a meeting to decide how to support her and wishes you a good new term with your classes. Feelings are briefly acknowledged, contained, parked, but given the importance that they deserve with time allocated later to the issue.

You enter your classroom, put on the best smile you can muster, make eye contact with students, comment on liking Sam's new hair style, mention that Ruby looks a bit down and offer to speak with her at lunchtime, ask Ali how his weekend was, thank Jack for opening the door for you, look round the class and say how good it is to see them all there and well done for making it to school on this rainy day! When they are all seated you might say that you are looking forward to a good day. You tell them you want to forget that you failed your driving test. It's so hard to be tested. You know how they feel, but like them you want to try again and not let the part of you that feels like giving up get the better of you.

Carrying the can

Being able to process our own feelings, and own them, is a very important pointer for children. They know we are human and vulnerable. We don't need to be automatons, but we do need to be the adult and let them be the child. In too many families children have felt responsible for the adults: responsible for their depression, their struggles. They may not show, it but that is not to say they do not feel it.

Below are some of the sad remarks children have made in conversation with me:

- 'If I was a better son/daughter, my parent would be happier.'

- 'If I had prevented them from drinking so much last night, they would not have lost their temper and hit out.'

- 'If I had been cleverer and not disappointed my parents, they would not have drowned their sorrows and got drunk and ended up fighting.'

- 'If I had not argued with my brother, he would not have gone out and stayed out all night. Now mum is so worried about him.'

Often these thoughts are hidden, and tragically the parents have no inkling that deep down this is what their children feel.

Taking responsibility as the adult can absolve the child and help prevent their descent into feeling a failure. Once a child feels they are inadequate, not capable enough, strong enough or clever enough, they can throw in the towel and get upset;

usually this is displayed as anger, and further battles ensue. The snowball effect of disillusionment is frightening. One small consequence can start an avalanche, and behaviour can cascade into defensive, aggressive misunderstandings. So many times I have asked myself, 'Whew, where did all that come from?' Small triggers can lead to large consequences.

Ways forward

Positivity breeds positivity

I was working with a young man Cameron, last year who was on the brink of exclusion from school. He had a quick trigger for feeling blamed, resulting in what seemed a seismic reaction to any form of correction. He was described by friends and teachers as 'often over-sensitive and over-reactive, but sometimes co-operative and hardworking'. I noticed that when he relaxed, and all was going well, he was pleasant, intelligent, open and funny but then suddenly he could slide into his inner morass.

I asked Cameron if he could describe to me the beginning of a good day and he replies:

'A good day, now let me think...well, my mum might come and tell me it's time to get up, and bring me a cup of tea. That would be an early morning. I like that because I can get myself together, find my uniform, pack my bag and so on. On a good morning I have time to eat. Eat breakfast: eggs and toast. I get the bus, get to school and see my mates, time to kick the football around before the bell goes.

'First lesson up on a good day, it's English – I like that. The teacher likes me. We often have a chat. She lives near me.

She knows I am good at football and going for trial. My spelling is not so good, but she helps me. I can ask for help whenever I like. Even if the next lesson is not one I like, I feel better, can face it, get to the end of the day. Go home with my mates. I might even do some homework.'

I thank Cameron for helping me understand. Am I right, I ask, that he likes to feel unrushed, to have time to organize himself, and appreciates a bit of T.L.C. from his mother, having her help him get up in time? He also likes to feel that a teacher notices him, that he exists as a person, not just a pupil, and that they are interested in his football career. He likes having a teacher who is willing to help and lets him ask for support when he is stuck.

'Uhuh, you got it!' he replies. This brightens his mood and motivates him. Understanding him was easy. Being able to be in a time and place to listen, when he would like to talk, was, as in all our lives, more difficult.

So how does a bad day start? Cameron goes on:

'Well now, that would be a day I over-sleep. Mum has gone to work early. I am supposed to listen to my alarm but have slept through. I know that bastard Mr F will give me grief. I forget my homework. Mrs S, she won't believe me that I did it. No time to eat. Grab some money, damn, missed the bus, walk to school. No point rushing now because I know I am in for it, detention for lateness. And then, just to top it all, Maths first lesson and Mr D hates me, he is on my case, I know it. No point trying, so I walk out. Another demerit. Then along comes Mr S. He just shouts. Always shouting, and in your face. Man, he should just back off. I hate that man. I just walk away, and he keeps saying, "Come back here." No point, I am out of there...spend the day on the street, wait to meet up with some other guys.'

I feel Cameron's dismay and frustration. I say:

'Waking up late makes a hard start to the day. It sounds as if not eating doesn't help your mood. That's quite normal for someone growing, like you. Lack of blood sugar can make us very wobbly. Then it can feel things go from bad to worse. I notice once you feel you will be in trouble for being late, it reminds you of other people who you struggle to feel are on your side. And then, if you have Maths, it's hard to trust that Mr D will help. I guess feeling we are failing makes it hard to try. Feeling we are not liked by someone makes it hard to be likeable. I imagine that a part of you on a day like this wants to walk away from the problem because you don't have enough good fuel of optimism in your tank. On a good day, which started well, you can face a bit of frustration and not give up.'

Cameron is smart. When not feeling threatened, he is quite reflective and honest. He sees how he presents as unlikeable to teachers if he is in a bad mood. This makes it hard for them to like him. It's not all their fault. He recognizes that he needs not to feel rushed in the mornings and determines to ask his mum to make sure he is awake before she leaves and to decide what he will eat for breakfast and leave it out the night before. He acknowledges how 'hangry' he gets without food and how he can be volatile and unreasonable. When reviewing his choices and behaviours, he feels more empowered.

The shroud of shame

So often children do want to be perfect and deep down are the worst critics of themselves. Cameron seems to have days when he communicates with a stony face, shrugging shoulders and dismissive scripts, but underneath this I realize he is prone to guilt and shame. Both feelings do damage as they are indigestible; for any of us they sit inside us and grow disproportionally. Shame is the worst as it can fall like a cloud and it's very hard to see from within a shroud. I remind myself to try to always avoid shaming a young person, especially as they have the least defence against this emotion, since already they are so critical of themselves.

Appreciation

Children crave positivity and, saying that, I think so do we all! There are easy gains in conversation with children in genuinely acknowledging what they do well. Sometimes we underestimate the damage that repetitive criticism or blame can do, the effects of living with the acid rain of negativity. We all learn best through praise, can feel better for sharing the joy of life, and tend to struggle with too much criticism (which can result in us either giving up or shutting down). It is well known in a range of learning contexts, from sports training to dog training, that praise builds confidence, and confidence facilitates learning new skills. When we feel empowered and effective, we do better. When we feel stupid, it increases our stupidity.

Cameron's teacher, Steve, is staying on the farm and sees the **power of encouragement**. He has become skilled at catching his pupils when they are being good. He reflects on how **reinforcing the negative only builds more negativity**. We talk about how patterns develop very quickly, and children will accept and play up to the labels that they are given. The child who is told from a young age that they are clumsy will become clumsier; the child who is labelled noisy will become louder; the teenager who is identified in the family as the lazy one will exhibit more idleness. We think about the labels that have been applied to this group he has brought by their teachers and parents. Labels can define people and make it hard to move away from the negative connotations.

...

Sarah is a teacher in a large, inner-city comprehensive school. It's the beginning of a new year. She wants to improve her relationship with tutees. She speaks of how some are slipping out of relationship with her, particularly a fragile girl called Jenny. What is going wrong?

Jenny is a people pleaser. She is shy and wants to be liked but is desperately under-confident. Her nails are bitten to the quick. She avoids eye contact and seems to have developed a twitch in her right eye. She is constantly late for school and late handing in homework, when previously she had been conscientious. Sarah wants to talk with her, to see if she can better understand what has changed in her life.

And then there is Sam. Sam is getting louder by the day. He is getting into fights at break and looking for trouble, and is yet seeming anxious when on his own and not surrounded by the banter of friends. Sarah is worried he is getting other teachers' backs up, and there is talk about him being excluded. She is perplexed. He did so well in Year 8. What has changed?

All these scenarios are going to take some skilful communication, listening and talking, to get to better understanding and find some potential positive ways forward. We consider some of the elements that help craft good communication and highlight some of the bear traps.

It seems Jenny is a child who bottles up her anxieties, is naturally untrusting and withdrawn, not given to much conversation. She seems to get by, by trying to go under the radar as if it is dangerous to put herself in full view. Her behaviours are powerful forms of communication. Jenny may be avoiding contact for many reasons. Sarah begins to think out loud:

'She may fear the world will be unkind and put her down if she talks. She may be so worried about something in her life and have internalized it so that the problem seems too huge to unpack. She may be used to being dismissed and over-ruled and having her thoughts and feelings minimized. She might have any number of scenarios going on in her life, from being a witness to domestic violence, being abused, bullied, blackmailed, or she might be being a carer and feeling overwhelmed, living with a parent with mental health issues, or neglected and never having been able to learn the social skills to survive in this big a school...'

Sarah is sensitive and picking up on overwhelm and rightly trying to imagine where Jenny's problems originate; but maybe right now she can just hold the thought that everything might feel too big for Jenny to know where to start.

Sam, on the other hand, seems to be struggling with self-control and aggression. His attention span is getting shorter, as is his fuse. He very easily walks out of class and over-reacts to any form of discipline. His reactions could be due to any of the sorts of questions that entered our mind about Jenny. **The disproportional responses** are different but could easily be his way of trying to cope with similar stressful situations. Perhaps both children are **drowning, not waving**. Sarah is aware she needs not to be too sucked in but be a reliable and patient support.

Both Jenny and Sam are unlikely to let us in to find out what is difficult in their lives if this becomes public property. Discretion is important, yet we cannot promise total confidentiality if the child is at risk. We need to find a good time and place that enables a chance to talk and listen yet does not feel too pressuring and intruding or too open and uncontained. We decide that Sarah can invite Sam to help carry books to her car: 'Sam, can I ask a favour? You are strong and energetic. Please could you lend me your help for five minutes?'

She could also ask Jenny, as the class are leaving: 'Jenny, I know you have a gerbil; can I ask your advice as I want to buy one for a friend? Maybe you would be kind enough to have a chat with me as I deliver this note to another classroom.'

Jenny is unlikely to be able to give much in an initial conversation. As with many children that might be harbouring a secret, she has put hours of time into carefully subconsciously creating a defence to protect herself. Why would she let go of this in an instant? We may with some children need to have saintly patience. We need to be willing to take the building of trust slowly but also be willing to show we are not shockable and are able to hear difficulties with neutrality. We are not going to take a chainsaw to rip apart the delicate fabric of her defences.

Both children may have a lot going on for them that they have struggled with but feel must remain hidden. They may be fiercely protective of the very people who are harming them. The parents or carers they have may be all that is available. Children grow up with the defects in their families and tend to absorb them rather than feel able to ask for help or complain publicly.

In my experience, it is common in cases where there are safeguarding concerns that it takes weeks or months for a child to build a secure enough relationship to disclose whatever it is that they are suffering from. Indeed, they may not see the issue as one of concern as after all it is their family's normal.

The language of concern is tricky. It is important we stay in step with the pace of the child in the levels of conversation. Sometimes it is like skilfully peeling the layers off an onion. Each one is delicate, almost transparent, and occasionally several layers come away together. We are walking alongside a child in awareness and can often comment on the real and obvious as a way of just acknowledging what we are seeing and hearing; but we do not need to interject too much of our feelings, and instead just show gentle curiosity and concern. For example:

'Sam, I experience you as so friendly, so I wondered what might have upset you when I saw you in a fight yesterday.'

'Jenny, you seem to work really hard at school and to be so conscientious, so I wondered if it is hard for you to get to school on time.'

Smoke screens may occlude the real reactions with the children. We must not be put off by them changing the subject or throwing in wild cards. Both Jenny and Sam may have turned the attention away from our concerns, but they will have registered a non-judgemental care.

Sam is the kind of child who may invite us into a relationship that is governed by the trading of insults, or confirmation of their being disliked. It takes practised deftness to sidestep this invitation and begin afresh with a different tone and intention. He is hypervigilant and reading all the body language. Before any words come out of our mouth, we are communicating a host of feelings and impressions. Consider how you feel when someone in authority comes into your space, face clouded with anger or, worse, distaste, with hostile **body language**, and begins to criticize you. I for one retreat inwardly and immediately start a defensive attack of thought about how unlikeable that person is. Often there is ongoing dialogue of wishful thinking about a retaliatory response. Internally we invent how in turn we could verbally humiliate and dent that person's inflated sense of self. How can I hurt them in the way I feel hurt? I am not open to dialogue or listening attentively. The tone alone can trigger that blocking response. **Tone** can denigrate, be competitive or authoritarian, or feel insulting and demeaning. Over-serious and humourless interactions can trigger feeling bored before the speaker begins; they are too intense and therefore impinging, and make you want to withdraw. Or the other person is simply too self-absorbed to leave room for you to feel free to think and respond in whatever way you need to.

Lecturing teenagers often backfires because they largely feel unheard and disrespected so zone out and miss anything constructive that might have been in the conversation. Moreover, a lecture from a parent or a teacher seldom includes any surprises. Children tend to know what we feel and therefore don't bother to listen to what we say when it's delivered as a lecture. It is easily done to resurrect some **feeling of being in control** as so often we feel we are floundering and awash with the same uncertainty the teenager may have. Holding forth, sounding reasonable, is often an unconscious reaction to the precariousness of the situation when we feel a child is beyond our control and we are desperate to restore some sense of order. Lecturing why something is dangerous may miss the point.

Often lecturing becomes sermonizing and the child's interest is lost. How often do we see an adult holding forth, energized by the sound of their own voice, sometimes needing an audience and failing to see they have lost the child's respect and attention? If possible, start on the same side, taking an interest in what they want to do, before polarizing and becoming oppositional.

Personal judgements. It is OK not to like some aspect of someone's behaviour but not to comment on them as a person. This can be interpreted as wholesale **assassination of character** so has to be discounted, or it may feel too painful to accept. We can often feel an entitlement to speak to a young person in a way we would never expect to get away with if it were an adult. An adult might fight back, physically or verbally. Why not a vulnerable teenager? Often young people tell me that they feel adults are hypocritical. They ask for respect but don't give it. Shouting at an adult the way you sometimes see an **adult hectoring** a child in school would be counted as **verbal abuse** or bullying. We need the same standards for our behaviour towards teenagers as we have for ourselves, however aggravating they are.

How many of us as adults feel contaminated by the legacy of someone's negativity? Sensitivity is not the preserve of adults alone; it's the landscape teenagers inhabit. They are struggling to feel 'good enough' by their own definition. As the adults, teachers or parents in their lives, we can wrongly assume a right to judge, define, label and insult.

Off on the wrong foot

How about a conversation that starts 'Mr Rolf was describing your bad behaviour to us in the staff room...'?

Second-hand criticism is not an auspicious beginning. Most of us hate to feel people are talking about us behind our back, especially if it is critical. It's that feeling of being **shamed** again. Any conversation that stimulates this response is going to have lasting toxicity. Resentment, defensiveness and anger might arise, and, if the intention is to help, you will be off to a bad start. A young person who feels defensive will also feel untrusting, and it is likely that conversations that trigger feeling disrespected will not end well!

Time can be a gift. Painfully, too late, I have had the feedback from my now adult middle child that he wanted more time and attention from us as parents. He seemed to be flourishing, self-motivated, busy, productive. Now I get the benefit of his honesty, that he wanted more: focus, listening to, even worrying about. I remember thinking that as a too busy parent I must stop to listen and try and make myself sit down, pay attention, focus. Yet, in general I was multi-tasking: parent, worker, homemaker. I can recognize how much I took him for granted; I was probably preoccupied and unfocused, both juggling and struggling.

Misguidedly I had thought teenagers liked to be independent and might need less of my time and preoccupations. How wrong I was. They may give the message that they don't care if you are around or not, do not want to be mollycoddled, resent having to take part in family activities and want to walk down the street at a distance, concealing any relationship to you; but deep down, teenagers are still very needy, very insecure, and need to be the ones who do the rejecting and distancing, not you. Being rushed seems to me to be a modern burden, especially in families where parents work full time, but it is harsh to pass this on to the children. This is a small window in their lives, never to be revisited, and they are not going to gratify us by thanking us for what feels like their right, as our children, to be given our time.

Metaphors and imagery can take the heat out of conversation and help avoid the bear trap of blame. They can be neutral and also involve a third position, thereby allowing space for reflection. Metaphors or images can be highly memorable. They can convey a huge narrative and expand in meaning by association within the young person's own mind. As metaphors and imagery require the use of the imagination to be understood they can be more easily associated with and less likely to be dismissed than bald factual statements. With the use of imagination, and in the crafting of this personal visualization, there is scope for free association and playfulness, with a lack of threat and predetermination. Using a metaphor shifts the gear and allows a child to engage another part of their brain; it connects them to the visceral or visual. It parks the problem and allows the vantage of a third position. It enables detachment from the energy of the 'problem' or conflict.

For some children, a description of them that is not confrontational may help:

- 'Joe, you seem unsettled, finding it hard to concentrate; you remind me of a bird hopping from plant to plant to gather seeds to eat.'

- 'Kamal, I'm curious that you are following Matthew's lead. I worry he might lead you over a cliff edge like lemmings do.'

- 'Tommy, you are like a great big battery, fully charged and ready to be used as an energy source.'

- 'Kim, you remind me of my phone when I forget to charge it. You might run right out of battery in a minute and switch off.'

Young people hate both **condescension** and **sarcasm**. Condescension, being spoken down to, is like a red rag to a bull and none of us, adult or child, like the feeling of being patronized. Sarcasm can make young people feel easily caught off-guard and confused. Confusion leaves them angry and upset, less available to thinking and reflectiveness. Sarcasm can be humiliating, and it is not fun to receive.

Children have taught me not to make too many assumptions and most of all to always be mindful of not creating confusion. Once we have a child on the back foot because they do not understand our vocabulary, we have lost their trust in the communication. Even thinking they cannot keep up with our use of language can let them feel disadvantaged, needing sometimes either to switch off or to denigrate the importance of the conversation wholesale.

Sharing feelings openly but with respect and ownership is a very different thing. Children hate secrets and half-truths; so if there is an issue that is concerning, it is better to find a constructive and honest way to talk about it. I have so often been amazed by children's ability to lie-detect. They have good instincts and often see though us; so honesty, with consideration of how much detail a child needs to know, is often the best policy. Ultimately children need to feel we can manage our lives, our emotions and our needs and not make them responsible for them.

The third position

I relish the opportunity to have a 'third position' to assist neutralizing conversations with young people. I think we can all relate to someone's attention feeling too intense, almost intrusive, embarrassing. Having another focus, a reason for being together, can make the space feel more manageable and relaxed.

Walking and talking, driving and talking, gardening and talking – all these can dilute the intensity. Sometimes it's better to have something to do to avoid too much intensity of eye contact and create another parallel agenda so the topic you need to focus on does not become too targeting. Neutral, shared territory helps create trust and balance by default. As a parent or teacher, it is helpful to have a parallel focus for attention, and conversation can develop and flow more naturally in and out of significant areas.

The arm wrestle: avoiding battles of wills

Young people are often adept at offering the invitation to fight, to argue. It is as if they toss down the gauntlet and invite us to duel. Sometimes they do this with subtlety and sometimes with rage, but there is so often a moment when we recognize the trap. Naming this process can help de-escalation or, even better, dilute the power of the process. Becoming conscious and aware gives us choices. We want children to be aware, but firstly we must see ourselves in the mirror, and be clear about the dynamics we are setting up and engaging in. It helps to 'think out loud': 'Ah, I see the offer of an argument here. It's tempting; I realize I easily fall into arguing, but I would rather not right now. I prefer to get along with you. I would rather try to understand.'

The potential for battles seems to be everywhere, every day. We can choose some. We cannot take them all on, and ideally need to win, so arm wrestling for power over issues that we cannot win may not be the best tactic: 'This battle of wills feels like a tug of war. I prefer to be on the same side. Maybe we don't need a winner. Can we pause? I might understand better if I take some time out.'

Tugs of war can only happen when both ends of the rope are being held under tension. It is easy to drop your end and the 'opponent' has no one to wrestle with. Better still, we can drop the rope and walk around to see the view from where our opponent is. If we join their team, there is no fight. It is the same with arguments: no resistance means there is no returning pressure.

It has been a privilege to listen to and have conversations with over 1000 children. If I have learnt one thing, it is that they long for understanding and crave approval, despite the behaviours that might indicate the opposite. Starting where they are, getting alongside before challenging, is always a good place to begin. Having a vocabulary of non-intrusive descriptors can help; open-ended statements are good places to start. For example:

- 'Maybe something has upset you.'

- 'You look troubled.'

- 'Perhaps something is bothering you.'

- 'I am wondering if you are feeling overloaded.'

- 'Perhaps some time out would help.'

For children refusing to engage, who struggle with emotional literacy, offers of alternatives can help: 'If number one is feeling rubbish and five is feeling good, I wonder where you might be?' Sliding scales can begin a conversation which may need a broader focus to feel safe. Sometimes a scale of one to ten helps for exploring any of the following feelings: frustrated, angry, upset, sad and fed up. Once the child is engaging, maybe we can try: 'I am curious to know if anything might help to bring up that number...' and 'Is there anything that brings you down?' The core of this is to discover what matters to this child, working towards how we might support them, what their needs might be.

Sometimes with younger children I employ a scatter technique: 'Tell me five to ten things that have upset you/made you angry/made you sad...' Usually by three or four the child begins to calm down, as they are letting off steam. Feelings are seldom single or uncomplicated. Causality is various. The order of importance in which we rank a child's needs or anxieties may not be the same as theirs. Over the years I have tried to learn to get closer to their own vision of the world, to be at their starting point and just for a while park my own theories and needs.

Conclusion

Sitting in the stairwell of a tower block in Camberwell in the semi-dark as the lights have broken and the lift is out of order, there is a strong smell of urine. I have a load of shopping I have got to take up to the eighth floor where my friend lives. No sleep last night as the neighbours were arguing, there were sirens in the street and my imagination ran rife. Should I call the police for that shout — it sounded like a young woman? In the stillness of the dark I wait for more clues. Maybe I am interfering, maybe I imagined it. The night is full of noises. I am never fast asleep, my antennae are on hyperalert and I am only here for one night. I am not sure of all this commotion. Is it my business or not? Sounds of lads joshing and feet on the pavement, and two large youths enter the lobby. My mind zip-wires fast between the knowledge there was a stabbing near here last week, fear that they might mug me, and wanting to be friendly. I have worked with kids from the secondary school around the corner and liked them all a lot. These lads could have been any of them, so why am I tinged with fear?

'Hi, it's a horrible night. Sorry to be blocking your way. I will move these bags of shopping – I just ran out of energy.' I smile, they stare, and then, 'It's no problem,' says the bigger lad, 'Can I help you carry your load?'

The ice is broken, my heart-rate slows, and together we mount the stairs, chatting about the weather and our respective days. They may be big, leather-jacketed, with jeans hung low, chains around their necks and lilting in slang speak, but they are still just teenagers and not the threat I imagined. We part on the landing outside my friend's door and I thank them for their kindness.

In London alone in 2018 there were 132 killings, and in 2019 there have been more.[1,2] Most of these deaths were teenagers. Violent crime is not confined to London but rife across the globe. I know this and so do they. This is the background that we are living in and it goes both ways. The boys are still children but living in an unsafe environment and treated with mistrust, and I realize that feeling safe is a privilege that most of them no longer have. Our society has become polluted by messages of fear, and adults and children alike are losing their trust to communicate the warmth and friendship that is vital to having a positive outlook on life. Teenagers are living tarred with this brush of being regarded as potentially dangerous, difficult or disturbed, and are becoming more isolated from their

....

1   BBC News (2018) 'London killings: all the victims of 2018.' Available at www.bbc.co.uk/news/uk-46128268 (accessed 08/04/2020).

2   G. Allen, L. Audicas, P. Loft and A. Bellis (2019) 'Knife Crimes in England and Wales.' Available at https://commonslibrary.parliament.uk/research-briefings/sn04304 (accessed 01/07/2020).

communities as a result. Society needs to stop vilifying them and give them a chance. We need to remember that teenagers are just like us, and crave feeling lovable and loved. Masks of indifference are only skin deep. I have seldom met a teenager who did not yearn to be discovered beneath that exterior.

Working with teenagers can be rewarding and challenging. But the bottom line is they need us to believe in them. If we regard them as a 'problem', they will no doubt fulfil our expectations. They all have huge potential and listening to them, I realize they are still hopeful that as adults we can help them. They are learning at a fast pace and we have to keep abreast. It is important we do not label them and restrict them in the confines of our imaginations. We need to let them teach us, surprise us and work with us. Above all, we need to include them, not exclude them.

Collaboration needs to be inter-generational

It should not all be down to individuals. Working and living with teenagers is tough. We talk about their resilience, but ours needs building too. The job of being a teacher, parent or social carer requires such emotional stamina to face the ascent and descent of a teenager's life. I am not sure many other jobs are tougher or require such agility of resourcefulness and patience! Donald Winnicott, the famous doctor and psychotherapist, spoke of the infant needing the father to hold the mother to hold the child.[3] Infant or teenager, the same applies, but for

....

3   D.W. Winnicott (1990) *Home Is Where We Start From: Essays by a Psychoanalyst.* Harmondsworth: Penguin.

many families this parental couple does not exist, and single parents are doing their best. If we can all support each other, we can create our own communities, families or tribes within which to hold the teenagers, but where adults feel held and backed up too.

Believing in the good in each other is a great place to start. While teenagers may act in ways that disturb us, dismay us, even denigrate us, holding on to what lies beneath that is the best way to survive. Although their moods can feel all-engulfing, it is important that we survive them. They need us to remain positive and know that their rejecting behaviour is only skin deep. Teenagers may act like they're invincible, but in fact they are fragile, and under the surface often conflicted. They are hungry for a sense of belonging and for nurture, a place they can identify themselves, often wanting to shrink and hide but ashamed they don't feel stronger. The strength of their emotion often equates to their underlying fear: fear of not being good enough, fear of growing up. They are caught between two worlds: childhood – a phase they may seem to want to demolish; and adulthood – their future, which deep down they know is not yet formed. They do not need us to remind them of their faults. Their priorities are not ours and if we try to hammer home our point of view, we risk alienating them further. They need us to take the time to understand their viewpoint and it is only then they might shift. As the world is feeling precarious, as if they are hanging on a cliff, they need us to throw a lifeline and let them gradually find a safe base.

Adult lives are often pressurized and it takes courage to identify our vulnerability. If we demonstrate that we understand we are fallible, it helps young people understand that to struggle is not a weakness. Openness is the root to healing wounds that otherwise would fester. But as with everything, there is balance, and our children need us to be sufficiently robust in order for them to feel they have a safe base. They are looking for signs of hope, so if there is a problem, it helps them to see we have determination to solve things and not give up. Teenagers often fear they are 'the problem' and their guilt can be triggered all too easily. They need to feel we will not give up on them, and this may mean we have to be the bigger person, to hold out an olive branch and always stay in touch. They look to us for safety, for continuity, for sense of a place in the world with values to live by. Surrounded by too much negativity in the world, they need us to be optimistic. Hopefulness, kindness and generosity are harbingers of joy. When teenagers are happier, they too can be tolerant, self-reflective, motivated and generous. Young people are hungry for the opportunity to change, and the opportunity to demonstrate the better parts of themselves. If we can craft these chances for them to shine, they reward us with their best.

Bibliography

Allen, G., Audicas, L., Loft, P. and Bellis, A. (2019) 'Knife Crimes in England and Wales.' Available at https://commonslibrary.parliament.uk/research-briefings/sn04304 (accessed 01/07/2020).

American Academy of Child & Adolescent Psychiatry (2016) 'Teen Brain: Behaviour, Problem Solving, and Decision Making.' Available at https://www.aacap.org/AACAP/Families_and_Youth/Facts_for_Families/FFF-Guide/The-Teen-Brain-Behavior-Problem-Solving-and-Decision-Making-095.aspx (accessed 18/06/2020).

Anderson, M. and Jiang, J. (2018) 'Teens, social media and technology 2018.' Available at www.pewresearch.org/internet/2018/05/31/teens-social-media-technology-2018 (accessed 31/01/2020).

Fader, S. (2019) 'Understanding the motivation: Why do people join gangs?' Available at www.betterhelp.com/advice/general/understanding-the-motivation-why-do-people-join-gangs (accessed 31/01/2020).

Gillet, T. (n.d.) 'Simplifying childhood may protect against mental health issues.' Available at http://raisedgood.com/extraordinary-things-happen-when-we-simplify-childhood (accessed 31/01/2020).

Gilmour, L. (2007) *Untangled: Running Our Race Without Being Sidelined by Emotions.* London: Blackwells.

Greene, R. (2014) *The Explosive Child.* New York, NY: Harper.

Hohnen, B., Gilmour, J. and Murphy, T. (2019) *The Incredible Teenage Brain*. London: Jessica Kingsley Publishers.

Holmes, J. (1993) *John Bowlby and Attachment Theory*. London: Routledge.

Holt, J. (1990) *How Children Fail*. Harmondsworth: Penguin.

James, W. (*producer*) (2008) *Life Outside Hackney* (video of the first visit to Jamie's Farm). Available at www.youtube.com/watch?v=iTyXXovYd00 (accessed 31/01/2020).

Jamie's Farm (2019a) 'It's not just about knives: Fear.' (Blog, 18 April) Available at https://jamiesfarm.org.uk/its-not-just-about-knives-fear (accessed 31/01/2020).

Jamie's Farm (2019b) 'The lure of gangs.' (Blog, 6 June) Available at https://jamiesfarm.org.uk/lure-of-gangs (accessed 31/01/2020).

Jamie's Farm (2019c) 'It's not just about knives: Solutions.' (Blog, 23 October) Available at https://jamiesfarm.org.uk/its-not-just-about-knives-solutions (accessed 31/01/2020).

Jamie's Farm (2019d) 'Adele's story.' YouTube film. Available at www.youtube.com/results?search_query=Adele+jamies+farm+ (accessed 31/01/2020).

Jamie's Farm (n.d.) https://jamiesfarm.org.uk/schools-teachers/podcasts/podcasts. Available at https://jamiesfarm.org.uk/blog-and-media.

Maslow, A.H. (1962) *Towards a Psychology of Being*. Connecticut, CT: Martino Fine Books.

Morgan, N. (2013) *Blame My Brain*. London: Walker Books.

Siegel, D. (2014) *Brainstorm: The Power and the Purpose of the Teenage Brain*. Scribe. New York, NY: Guildford Press.

Siegel, D.J. and Hartzell, M. (2005) *Parenting from the Inside Out, Tenth Anniversary Edition: How Deeper Self-Understanding Can Help You Raise Children Who Thrive*. New York, NY: Penguin.

Sunderland, M. (2015) *Conversations That Matter*. Duffield: Worth Publishing.

TrackMyStack (n.d.) '6 Symptoms of Low Dopamine.' Available at https://trackmystack.com/articles/6-symptoms-low-dopamine (accessed 18/06/2020).

Weir, K. (2014) 'The lasting impact of neglect.' *The Journal of the American Psychological Association 45*, 6, 36.

Winnicott, D.W. (1990) *Home Is Where We Start From: Essays by a Psychoanalyst*. Harmondsworth: Penguin.

Winnicott, D.W. (2006) *The Family and Individual Development*. London: Routledge Classics.

Winnicott, D. 'The "Good-enough" Mother Radio Broadcast.' *The Collected Works of D.W. Winnicott*. Edited by Lesley Caldwell and Helen Taylor Robinson. Oxford: Oxford University Press.

Young Minds (2018a) 'New Figures on CAMHS Waiting Times.' Available at https://youngminds.org.uk/blog/new-figures-on-camhs-waiting-times (accessed 17/06/2020).

Young Minds (2018b) 'YoungMinds Trusts, Annual Reports and Accounts, Year ended 31 March 2018.' Available at https://youngminds.org.uk/media/2757/youngminds-annual-report-2017-18.pdf (accessed 18/06/2020).

Index

Printed in Great Britain
by Amazon